M000002995

O Canada!

Historical Narratives and Biographies That Tell

Her Story

Karla Akins

BRAMLEY BOOKS
www.bramleybooks.com

A Division of Knowledge Quest, Inc.
An Oregon Corporation

Published by BRAMLEY BOOKS
A Division of Knowledge Quest, Inc.
P.O. Box 789
Boring, OR 97009
www.knowledgequestmaps.com

Written by Karla Akins
Cover Design by Cathi Stevenson
Maps designed by Greg Joens
All photos used are in the public domain

Printed in the United States of America
Copyright © 2011 Knowledge Quest, Inc.
All rights reserved
ISBN # 978-1-932786-45-3

This book is sold subject to the condition that it shall not, by way of trade or other-wise, be lent, re-sold, hired out, or otherwise circulated without the publisher's prior consent in any form of binding or cover orther than that in which it is published and without a similar condition being imposed on the subsequent purchaser.

Publisher's Cataloging-in-Publication data

Akins, Karla.

     Oh Canada! : historical narratives and biographies that tell her story / written by Karla Akins
     p. cm.
     ISBN 978-1-932786-45-3

     Contents: Jada: Girl of Haida Gwaii -- Bjorn the Lundehund -- The Old Violin -- Lucy Maud Montgomery -- The Discovery of Insulin by Sir Frederick Grant Banting -- The Dionne Quintuplets -- Canada's School on Wheels -- Canada's Hero: Terry Fox.

                                  PCN 2011937499

This book is dedicated in loving memory of my precious Grandmother,
Leota Fredericka Pratt,
who kept me knee deep in oatmeal raisin cookies as a kid
while I pounded out stories on an old typewriter perched
atop a wobbly aluminum TV tray table.
Thanks, Grandma. I miss you.

Dear Reader,

The main facts in these stories are true. I have taken liberties with dialogue and plot details to make them interesting for young readers.

No one is perfect. Some of the people portrayed in these stories had character flaws that were not featured in the stories I told. Instead I focused on their positive qualities and chose to leave it to the reader's curiosity to learn more about each person's foibles and weaknesses.

I love to hear from my readers. Please e-mail me through my website: http://KarlaAkins.com.

Happy Reading!

Karla Akins

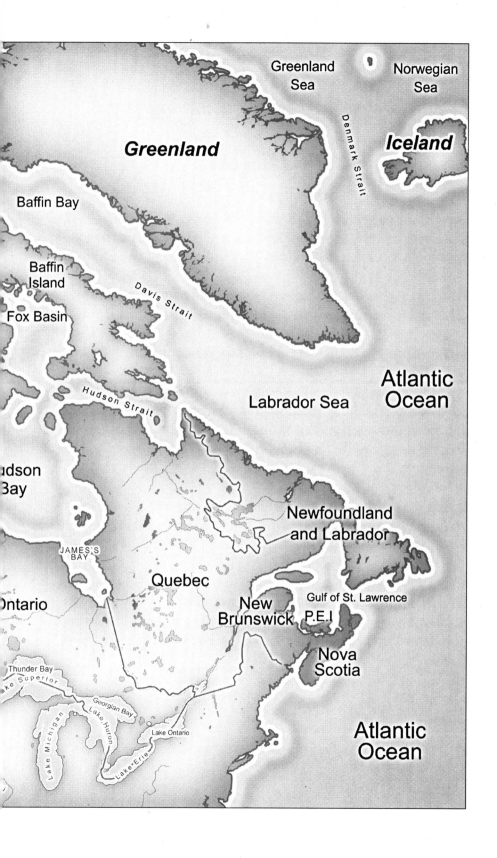

Acknowledgements:

I have many people to thank for the production of this book. First, all praise goes to my Father God, my Savior Jesus Christ and the precious Holy Spirit, Who inspires and teaches me day by day, word by word.

Next, I want to thank my husband, Eddie and my children still at home, Isaiah and Isaac, for allowing me the time to write. While I'm in my "writing cave" they're forced to scrounge for meals and clean clothes on their own. Their patient longsuffering during my writing hibernation is a huge blessing.

I also want to thank my gifted writing buddies (all award-winning authors themselves) for their invaluable input: Camille Eide, Emily Hendrickson, Jennifer Kaufeld, Linda Glaz, Cheryl Martin, and Jessica Nelson.

Thanks must also go to my publisher, Terri Johnson, at Bramley Books, who came up with the idea for this book and trusted me to write it. She is a dream to work with. Thank-you, Terri!

And to all people who have helped me along the path of my writing career, but aren't mentioned because of lack of space or my great absent-mindedness, thank-you for your encouragement and for believing in an awkward, quirky writer. I give you my heart-felt appreciation and thanks.

TABLE OF CONTENTS

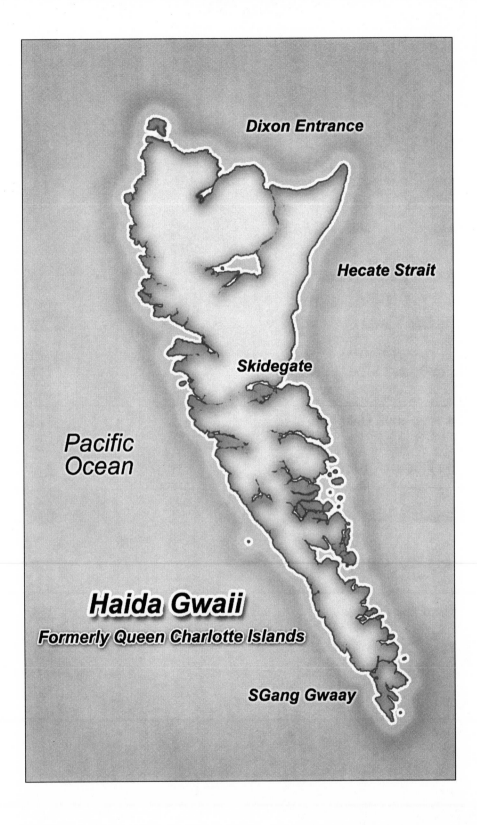

Dixon Entrance

Hecate Strait

Skidegate

Pacific
Ocean

Haida Gwaii
Formerly Queen Charlotte Islands

SGang Gwaay

Jada: Girl of Haida Gwaii

I sat behind my grandfather, inches from the water, as we paddled away from his touring boat, The Haanas. Our kayak matched the hue of the clear, sapphire sky. The water, like a faultless, smooth mirror, reflected the colours of my red vest and tawny skin.

At the edge of small rocky islands, seals slipped in and out of silvery marine pools and basked in the sun. Seal pups cried out for their mothers and wallowed along the brim of the deep. Grandfather pointed to a pod of humpback whales farther out in the Pacific Ocean. One breached the water as if to say, "Welcome home, Jada; we have missed you."

It waved its enormous tail fluke and returned to the shining waters to protect the calves who swam close to their mothers. The humps of their backs glinted in the morning sun, and their blow holes sprayed the morning sky with a mist of salutation.

Grandfather and I did not speak. He gestured with his eyes and hands in the direction of what I needed to see. He pointed at cobalt blue and scarlet starfish decorating the rocks in the water below, among palm-sized red rock crabs scuttling through patches of seaweed that looked like the lettuce in my grandmother's garden. White-cap limpets, red-turban snails, and gleaming blue-top snails clung to kelp and rocks. Among them, giant plumose anemones, sea urchins in violet, crimson and blue, and mysterious-looking neon nudibranchs lived like a kaleidoscope under crystal-clear glass.

Grandfather touched my shoulder and pointed far off into the distance, where Dall's porpoises swam beside a touring boat while people stood on the bow taking pictures. I reached for my cell phone and took pictures of a flock of puffins sitting on rocks not far from our kayak. I wanted to send the pictures to my parents in Prince George, on the mainland. My mother's favourite bird, besides the raven, was the puffin.

One day, while finishing my school report on Canadian history, my mother walked into my room and said, "You will spend the springtime and summer with your grandfather." She spoke to me in her native Haida tongue, "You need to remember your heritage."

I grinned and teased my mother, "How can I cross the ocean by myself? I'm not an Orca; I'm a Haida girl."

Mother giggled and looked towards Father, who was studying for Sunday's sermon.

"Grandfather will come in his float-plane[1] and get you. It's the only way to the islands of your ancestors."

This is why I found myself happily paddling behind my grandfather in a kayak, on the beautiful waters of Haida Gwaii.

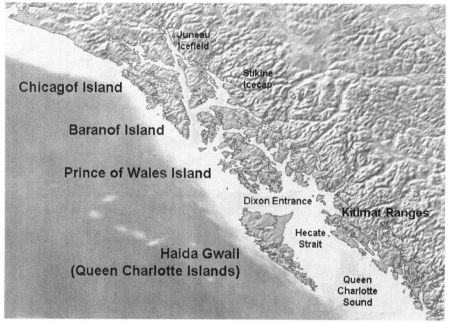

Image: Wikimedia / Public Domain / Haida Gwaii in Western Canada

Grandfather waited patiently as I took pictures and wrote a text for my parents. I did not think I would get reception out here, but the message would be saved in my phone for when I could send it later. After I finished, we rowed on towards the island of my forefathers. No sound was heard except the rhythm of our paddles dipping like hot spoons into Grandmother's mushroom soup. Beside us, along the banks of a small island, sea otters yawned and woke from their nighttime sleep. They slid into the cold, silent water with less sound than the slurps of our paddles. I stifled a giggle as they played peek-aboo with their tiny, otter hands and washed their sweet, expressive faces.

Grandfather pointed with his paddle across the way at a black bear, or taan, "brother of man," lumbering across a rocky shore in the morning mist. He fished for breakfast as bald eagles peered at us from the limbs of trees . I remembered what Grandfather taught me yesterday about these creatures: brother bear of Haida Gwaii has stronger jaws than any other bear because he must crush shells with his teeth. He is the largest of the black bears in North America, and I was proud to know him.

Quietly, we paddled towards the north end of the island of SGang Gwaay and pulled our kayak to rest on its rocky shore.

"Grandfather, tell me the story of the boy of Beringia," I entreated softly as he had taught me. Living in the city of Prince George, I rarely thought of my brothers, raven and eagle, but here, grandfather taught me that I shared the land with all creatures, and must respect them.

"How many times must I repeat this tale, Jada?" Grandfather teased. I knew he liked telling me the story. After we unpacked our lunch, we stood like cedars on the banks of the hidden cove and peered out at the clear, still waters. It was becoming an unusual day. Normally, the weather was misty, rainy, and cold. Today the sun shone and the mist lifted to the tops of trees, revealing snow-peaked mountains atop islands in the distance.

I smiled at my grandfather and handed him one of my grandmother's biscuits. "You must repeat the Haida stories so I can

12

remember to tell my children. My memory is short."

Grandfather nodded and mumbled, "I will tell you the story this time, but tomorrow night at the potlatch, it will be your turn to tell it."

"Me? But Grandfather, I…"

"Yes, you. You are the great-great-granddaughter of a chief. Much is expected. Tomorrow you will take your place among the others as my only grandchild. Our people must have assurance that the stories will not die."

"Oh, *Chinaay*," I tickled him under his chin. "Grandfather, you will never die. You are too wise and feisty."

He laughed and spread a small tarp on the damp ground for us to sit upon, before our hike to the other side of the island.

"First we rest and eat. When we get to the totems, I will tell you the story."

Looking out at the cove, there was much to observe. Since arriving, I hadn't missed my television or wanted to play my video games. My eyes didn't seem big enough nor my mind large enough to behold all the animals and plants on the remote, island archipelago of Gwaii Haanas. I chewed my biscuit and smiled, remembering the Orcas we saw yesterday as we kayaked through island waters. If only my friends could see the Steller sea lions, raptors, and sea birds I now knew. Things would seem different to me back home in Prince George.

I decided to try and talk my parents into moving back to these islands. YouTube and Facebook seemed a lifetime away, and I am only fourteen years in this world. Posting on Facebook and my blog about shoes and shopping at the mall seemed silly now. All my friends needed to see Gwaii Haanas: "Place of Wonder." I took plenty of pictures and recorded enough videos to post online every day for a year. I promised myself to post all things Haida Gwaii from now on, in honour of my ancestors.

If my friends could see me now in my wetsuit, with my messy hair, they would be shocked. Without being here with me, they would not understand what I learned on this sanctuary. Grandfather told me there are more than thirty-nine species of animals unique to this archipelago, and I saw many of them. These beautiful isles were Canada's own "Galapagos." Sometimes I could not believe I was a Haida child and blessed enough to see it all.

"We have been given unusually clear weather today," declared Grandfather as he brushed the crumbs from his lap and stood. "Someone wants you to know all there is to learn here. You would do well to pay close attention, *Aljuu*, Dear One."

Grandfather was right. It rained often here, in the rainforest biome of these islands. The temperature and weather fluctuated from morning until night. We packed our things into the kayak and headed towards the boardwalk, leading between enormous western hemlock, sitka spruce, and western red cedar trees. Thick, curvy, exposed roots covered in moss wound their long tentacles along rocks and hills, creating spooky walls of shadow and light. Tree limbs beckoned us to enter the island and learn of its hidden secrets. A shiver crept up my arms, and I reached for grandfather's hand as we neared the cabin of the Watchman, a friend of my grandfather.

"Welcome back to Sgang Gwaay, Bill!"

It startled me to hear someone call my grandfather "Bill." I never thought about him having friends who called him by his first name.

I whispered in my grandfather's ear, "What does Sgang Gwaay mean?"

The Watchman overheard my question.

"It means Red Cod Island Town. Early traders called it by the name of our chief 'Koyah', and others called it 'Nunsting,'" he explained as he smiled and reached to hug my grandfather.

Grandfather embraced the Watchman.

"Hello, Jordan. I'm here to introduce my granddaughter to her ancestors."

"You know the way," Jordan smiled, "or do you want the tour?"

Grandfather laughed. He too was a Watchman, one who took care of the islands set aside as Park Reserves. He gave tours and did not need a guide. Sgang Gwaay was special. It was a World Heritage Site.[2] No one is allowed to traverse the island without a Watchman from the Haida tribe.

Jordan bent down and whispered into my ear, "Beware of ghosts. To walk among the totems is to feel the presence of your ancestors who carved them and lived beside them. While they stand, they still live."

Another shiver ran up my spine, and I squeezed Grandfather's hand harder. His smile assured me, and we marched forward to the shore of my forefathers. We walked a great distance through thick grass and mossy trees, before reaching a cave.

"It is here where many Haida lived and were buried," whispered Grandfather, as he stood silently bowing his head and murmuring words in Haida I did not understand. I knew he was praying.

Finally, we reached the far shores of Sgang Gwaay, where tall cedar totems stood facing a sheltered cove, looking like weary soldiers, prepared to defend the island. I felt sorry for them. They were warped, tilted, and weather-beaten but seemed strong and proud. Moss peeked out of crevices, and parts of them were broken and badly splintered. Some of their carvings were missing, especially at the top. It upset me.

"Grandfather, why don't the Watchmen take better care of these totems? They're falling apart."

"No, my child. They're returning to the earth from whence they came. It's as it should be."

"Then why are they here? What do they mean?"

"Each totem tells a specific story, and each image has a specific meaning: a wedding, a death, or a great battle. I can't tell you which, because those who know are people now long gone."

I took my camera out of my backpack and snapped pictures. Would my children be able to see these totems? Or would they be gone? Vowing to keep the pictures safe allowed me the luxury of

16

passing the stories on to my own children.

CB

"This used to be the entrance to our village." Grandfather spread his arms and pointed to the shore protected by other islands and trees. "Long before white men came. Long before the great sickness."

"Was that before or after the boy of Beringia's journey?"

I craned my neck to see the carvings of animals, birds, frogs and other creatures on the tall totems. Grandfather followed me as I snapped pictures of them.

"No, it happened after the journey. The boy of Beringia was much longer ago."

I stopped taking pictures of the totems and snapped one of Grandfather looking up into the face of a carved whale.

"Tell me the story again, Grandfather."

Grandfather sat on the grass in front of the totems and faced them, as if he were going to have a council meeting. I sat beside him and looked at these proud, solitary beams. Loneliness slipped inside my skin, and I could almost hear its cries for what had happened on this island.

"Long ago, these islands did not exist. They were part of the mainland of North America. There were no trees. Ice covered most of North America, and there was land connecting it to Siberia , because the seas were much lower. We call that land 'Beringia.' It's all under water now."

"I've read about the land bridge in my history book," I nodded. "But some people don't believe there was a Beringia."

Grandfather smiled and confessed, "Some of our people don't either, but I call this particular story 'The Boy of Beringia' to help you understand, young Jada. These islands were once at least twice as large as they are today. Our people lived along the shore to be close to salmon, seals, and other foods from the sea."

I looked up at Grandfather, and he smiled down at me and patted my arm.

"You see, our stories, passed down from generation to generation, speak of ice and snow that did not melt and flow back to the oceans. The snow became giant glaciers and more of the earth's water stayed on the land than in the ocean. We speak of a small passage between two ice sheets and journeys by canoes along the shores of the Pacific. It is through these passages the Haida traveled. We were the first ones. The sea in those days was not as high. Hecate Strait was dry land."

How wonderful it must have been to see such glaciers and live on such land.

"Did it snow?"

"No, it didn't snow. Beringia was arid. During the Ice Age, there were always parts of Beringia that were cold with little snow or ice."

I rested my head on grandfather's shoulder and closed my eyes, imagining the story he told.

Grandfather stroked my hair and continued, "In those days,

18

there was a boy named Scannah-gan-nuncus. He was an adventurous boy – about your age – and he enjoyed exploring in his canoe more than anything. Our people, Jada, were great canoe-makers from long, long ago. Before there were trees, we made our canoes from the skins of the great animals that roamed here with us."

I looked up at Grandfather and the sea air brushed my face. I realized that the same salty air weathered the totems.

"What sorts of animals?"

"Many kinds: caribou, musk-ox, mammoth, and mastodon. It was cold then. We wore animal-fur clothes to keep warm, much as our brothers, the Inuit do today. Not much food grew on this land, except for hardy grasses, herbs, dwarf birch, and willows to feed the herds of animals. The horse, mountain sheep, saiga antelope, and musk-ox clothed and fed us."

"Were there other animals besides those? My history teacher says there were many animals but they're extinct now," I yawned and snuggled closer to Grandfather.

"Your teacher is correct. There were camels, short-faced bears, American lions, and scimitar cats. Some of our people followed herds of mammoth and bison, and they led us here. Others of our people came by skin-canoes and fished for capelin and smelt, squid, crab, and lobster. But most of us believe we were the first peoples on earth."

"Where did they live? There were no trees for houses."

"We sometimes lived in caves, but we also gathered twigs from bushes and built small houses with skins."

"Is this how Scannah-gan-nuncus lived, too?"

I wanted Grandfather to tell me more about this mysterious boy.

Grandfather nodded, "This is how Scannah-gan-nuncus lived, except that by the time he was born, there were trees on the land. He was adventurous, and his father kept him busy making tools from obsidian that we now call micro-blades. He also enjoyed fishing for eulachon, herring, and halibut, exactly as we do today."

I sat up.

"I heard about micro-blades at the heritage center. They found some right here on this island, in a cave."

"That's right, Jada. Once our people settled here along these beautiful waters, we no longer needed to constantly hunt big game. Instead, we fished and harvested shellfish and sea creatures."

"That must have taken a long time, hunting for food."

I thought about how easy it was for me to go to the store to get my groceries.

"Actually, it didn't. In fact, the food was so plentiful that the Haida had plenty of time left for art and music. Many other tribes, farther away from the sea, did not have as much time for these things because they needed to hunt in order to eat and constantly moved when the animals moved. We settled here and had instant access to food from the sea."

"Like an ice age drive up window," I giggled.

Grandfather chuckled, "Yes, something like that, but we also needed clothing, and so we hunted mountain goats, beaver, seals, sea

20

lions, and sea otters."

"Oh, not sea otters!" I frowned.

"Yes, they too provided us with warm clothes and food when it was too cold to fish. We're grateful to them." Grandfather pulled at a blade of grass and sucked on it.

"And to the God who made them?"

I looked at Grandfather from the corner of my eye. My parents believed differently from Grandfather. He worshipped nature. My parents worshipped the God of nature. It caused friction between my parents and my grandparents, but I didn't want it to cause distance between Grandfather and me, too.

Grandfather was silent, and he looked up at the sky.

"I only know what my ancestors have taught me, Jada. Sometimes I wish I hadn't let your mother go to that school of the Christian God."

I sighed. It made me sad that Grandfather did not want to hear about my God, but he wanted me to know about his. I said a silent prayer. Maybe someday God would open his ears to hear my words, but for now, I would listen and learn the things Grandfather was teaching me. It was the Holy Spirit's job to reach him. I needed His wisdom to know what to say.

I changed the subject.

"Did the boy of Beringia eat vegetables?"

"Of course! He ate ferns and seaweed, berries and camas bulbs, and your grandmother's mushroom soup."

"Grandmother's soup? Is Grandmother that old?"

Grandfather laughed and slapped his leg, "No, but her soup is. Haida Gwaii rainforest chanterelles have been here from the beginning."

"All the mushrooms?"

I had seen some growing on a tree on our way to the totems. If I could, I would eat them on the way back.

"No, not all of them. Some are poisonous. There is plenty of food here in the forests of Haida Gwaii. In the springtime, we eat seaweed, clams, and salmon or halibut. In the summertime, Grandmother picks wild berries, garden vegetables, and oyster mushrooms on alder logs."

"Like the ones I saw along the trail?"

My mouth watered thinking of Grandmother's stew, and my stomach growled.

"Yes. See? Your eyes are Haida, even if your father is not."

Grandfather's eyes grew somber. I could tell it still bothered him that my mother had married my father, a pastor in Prince George.

I tried to distract him with more questions.

"What do you eat in the fall?"

Grandfather blinked and leaned back on his elbows.

"That's when Grandmother hunts for chicken of the woods mushrooms, porcini mushrooms, and hedgehog mushrooms, as well as her favourite: wild orange chanterelles."

"If they're Grandmother's favourite, then they're my favourite too."

22

I leaned back on my elbows beside Grandfather and stared at a totem with the face of a bear.

"If the boy of Beringia had plenty of food, why did he travel a long distance from home?"

"I don't know. As I said, he was an adventurous boy. Perhaps he wanted to see what he could find to do elsewhere. But he sailed far up the Hunnah, a mountain stream that emptied its waters into the Skidegate channel. In those days, the river was much larger. Today, there isn't enough water to float a canoe unless the water is high.

"After rowing upstream most of the day, his arms grew tired, and he decided to eat the lunch his grandmother had made for him. He pulled his canoe ashore and rested on big boulders on the side of the stream. Along the edge of the river was timber. While resting, he heard a terrible sound approaching. He had never heard such a sound before. He looked up and saw all the stones in the river coming towards him. He was terribly frightened, jumped to his feet, and ran. Scannah-gan-nuncus ran into the trees, but they were cracking and groaning and shouting to him, 'Go back! Go back at once to the river and run as fast as you can!'"

"Did he?"

"He did. But he was a curious, hasty boy; he wanted to see what was crushing the stones and breaking the trees. He went back and found a large body of ice coming down the river, pushing everything before it. Finally, he got into his canoe and paddled home as quickly as he could."

"And that's why this is an island now?"

I looked around at the trees and totems and imagined the boy of Beringia here.

Grandfather sat up and answered, "Yes, and proof our people were here from the beginning."

"I'm glad the boy of Beringia made it safely home. Do you have other stories?"

"Have I told you the one about the Flood-Tide Woman?"

"No."

"Would you like to hear it?"

"Of course, *Chinaay*, you're teasing me."

Grandfather put his arm around me and hugged me closer to him. I listened to his rich, deep voice with the native lilt of the Haida tongue. I could listen to him for hours. I wish I did not have to return home to Prince George.

"Once long ago, a crowd of boys and girls played on the beach. At the water's edge, they saw a strange woman wearing a fur cape.

"A little boy walked up to her to learn who the stranger was. The other children followed him.

"The boy pulled up her cape, exposing her backbone. Sticking out of her spine was a plant, called 'Chinese slippers,' that grows on the seashore. This made the children laugh and jeer. When the old people heard the children's clamor, they told them to stop laughing at the stranger. At that moment the tide was at its low ebb. The woman sat down at the water's edge, and the tide began to rise, touching her

24

feet. She moved up the shore a little and again sat down. The water rose, and again she moved higher. Finally, she sat down at the edge of the village.

"The tide kept rising; never before had it come so high. The villagers grew frightened and awe-struck.

"They had not yet learned how to build canoes and didn't know how to escape, but they took big logs, tied them together into a raft, and placed their children on it. They packed the raft with dried salmon, halibut, and baskets of spring water for drinking.

"Meanwhile, the stranger kept sitting down, and, when the tide came up to her, she moved away to higher ground, up the hillside, up the mountain. Many people saved themselves by climbing onto the raft with the children. Others made more rafts, until there were a number afloat.

"The whole island was now covered by the sea, and the hundreds and hundreds of survivors were drifting without being able to stop, since they had no anchors. By and by, the people saw peaks sticking out of the ocean. One of the rafts drifted to a piece of land, and its survivors stepped off there, while other rafts were beached elsewhere.

"That is when the tribes became dispersed. Those who landed here are the Haida, your people, Jada. You are of the Raven clan because your mother is a Raven. A Raven clan member must not marry a Raven. You must marry an Eagle."

"Grandmother is a Raven, and you are an Eagle?"

"That's right."

"That flood story, Grandfather, sounds much like the story of Noah of the God of the Bible. Would you like to hear that story?"

Grandfather smiled down at me.

"Maybe someday."

We sat in silence for awhile and stared up at the great totem poles. After a few moments in our own thoughts, Grandfather spoke:

"Long ago, the early Haida buried their chiefs by putting their bodies into a wooden box, which was placed at the top of a burial totem in front of the chief's lodge. The carvings tell the story of significant events in his life."

"Are all the poles burial totems?"

Grandfather shook his head and rose to his feet. He reached out his hand to help me up.

"No, there are clan poles with figures of bears, eagles, ravens, and lots of other animals. Sometimes we raise a pole in memory of a chief. And there are shame and welcome totems."

"I think I know what a welcome totem is, but what's a shame totem?"

"We made shame totems to punish someone who committed a shameful or dishonourable act. We carved a pole and displayed it publicly to shame that person. Once the person had made restitution, the pole could be taken down and burned."

Grandfather and I walked among the totems. The wind in the trees sounded like the whispers of my ancestors, telling me they were glad to see me and I should come more often.

Grandfather's voice startled me out of my daydream.

"Some of our people used totem poles as house supports. If the tribe moved, these totem poles were small enough to be transported and used in a new dwelling."

He pointed to giant beams connected together, lying in disarray and covered in moss.

"These are all that remain of our village and the great long houses."

I walked towards the long house beams and imagined the great dwelling that once stood here.

Grandfather took a deep breath and turned back to the totems.

"Do you still make scrapbooks with your mother?"

"Of course! You know how much my mother loves to scrapbook. She makes beautiful memory albums."

"A totem pole can be like a family's scrapbook. It's a history book showing how people are related to one another; or they can tell a family joke."

"A joke?"

I smiled and gazed up at the totems and tried to imagine my ancestors telling a joke.

Grandfather grinned, "Yes. The Haida love to tell stories to make people laugh, but the totems also tell secret stories that only the family knows, and no one else will ever know."

 beta

"What happened to this village? Why are there no longer people here?"

"In 1862, when some of our people encamped at Victoria to trade, ships brought white men with small pox to the city. When our people got the disease, the white men refused to heal us even though they knew how. They had vaccines. They knew how to quarantine us. Instead, they sent our sick back to our villages, here on Haida Gwaii, pulling twenty of our canoes behind their gunboat, *The Forward*. The sick infected nearly everyone in the village and almost everyone died. You are the daughter of the ones who lived."

"Why would they do such a thing to us? What had we done?"

Grandfather pulled a sheet of paper out of his pocket, unfolding it.

"We were First Peoples: Indians. That's all. Between 1774 and 1874, nine-tenths of our people died of diseases and from firearms and liquor. It was a century of mourning, as every Haida family lost someone. Entire families died. We had twenty villages, and then we only had seven. Later, there were only two."

I was speechless. The numbers of which Grandfather spoke were too many for me to grasp. He reached into his pocket and brought out an old, tattered piece of paper. He unfolded it carefully and handed it to me. I took it from him and read:

July 7, 1862, The Daily British Colonist:

"The small pox seems to have exhausted itself, for want of material to work upon; and we have heard of no new cases [of smallpox infecting Victoria's residents] within the last few days. One or two Indians die nearly every day; but what is an Indian's life worth? Not so much as a pet dog's, to judge from the cruel apathy and stolid indifference with which they were allowed to rot under the very eyes ... of those whose sacred duty it was to have comforted them in their hour of misery and wretchedness."

Through tears, I fixed my eyes on the totems and imagined my people here, raising their families, fishing, gathering mushrooms, and telling stories. I imagined their potlatches and ceremonies, during which they danced and sang songs. I could practically hear their cries from across the waters, where they fished for food and raced their canoes among the porpoises and the whales.

Grandfather unfolded another sheet from his pocket and read it to me:

" 'What will they say in England?' when it is known that an Indian population was fostered and encouraged round Victoria, until the small-pox was imported from San Francisco. They, when the disease raged amongst them, when the unfortunate wretches were dying by scores, deserted by their own people, and left to perish in the midst of a Christian community that had fattened off them for four years – then the humanizing influence of our civilized Government comes in – not to remedy the evil that it had brought about – not to become the Good Samaritan, and endeavour to ameliorate the effects of the disease by medical exertion, but to drive these people away to death, and to disseminate the fell disease along the coast. To send with them the destruction perhaps of the whole Indian race in the British Possessions on the Pacific ...There is a dehumanizing fatuity about this treatment of the natives that is truly horrible ... How easy it would have been to have sent away the tribes when the disease was first noticed in the town, and if any of the Indians had taken the infection, to have had

a place where they could have been attended to, some little distance from Victoria, until they recovered as they in all probability would have done with medical aid. By this means the progress of the disease would at once been arrested, and the population saved from the horrible sights, and perhaps dangerous effects, of heaps of dead bodies putrifying [sic] in the summer's sun, in the vicinity of town ... The authorities have commenced the work of extermination – let them keep it up ... . Never was there a more execrable Indian policy than ours."[3]

(Daily Press, June 17, 1862 .)

Grandfather folded up the paper and placed it in his pocket. He stared out to sea.

"You're angry, aren't you grandfather?"

I could see pain in his eyes.

He nodded.

"I carry these papers with me, so I won't forget," he replied as he looked down at me and placed his hand on my shoulder. "And you must not forget, either, little Jada."

"I'm not too little anymore, Grandfather," I assured him as I put my hand over his. "And I won't forget, but I choose to forgive."

Grandfather shook his head and firmly stated, "Then you do not understand the suffering of our people."

"No, Grandfather, I do understand . I will tell my children all you've taught me, but because I've been forgiven of much, I choose to forgive. It's the only way to heal."

"What could you, a young child, need to be forgiven for?"

"We all need forgiveness."

Grandfather stood silent. I understood now, why Grandfather was upset with my mother for marrying outside our tribe, and for accepting the Christian God. I wanted him to understand me and my beliefs, as much as he wanted me to understand his – ours.

Grandfather stood with his hands in his pockets, looking out at the horizon and sighed, "At least they no longer call this place the Queen Charlotte Islands."

"Why did they call it that anyway?"

No queen lived here.

Grandfather stroked the side of a totem and explained, "The islands were named after the HMS Queen Charlotte, Lord Howe's flagship, named in honour of Queen Charlotte, wife of King George III. For King George's Sound Company, the flagship traded in sea otter furs between the Pacific coasts of America and China."

I covered my face.

"Oh, not my sea otters again!"

Grandfather chuckled, "Yes, Jada, your beloved sea otters were a valuable commodity in those days. And because of his ventures here in 1787, Captain George Dixon named these beautiful islands after his vessel."

"But my great-grandfathers, they called this place Xhaaidlagha

32

Gwaayaai—Islands at the Boundary of the World."

I liked the feel of the Haida words rolling off my tongue.

Grandfather grinned. I think he was proud I remembered.

"That's right. And do you remember the ceremony on June 17, 2010?"

Only days before, Grandfather had taken me to the ceremony that restored our beautiful islands to their Haida name. In the Aajii kyee gan saa guudang aas.uu sahlgaan dang ga t'alang isdaang – Yahguudang dangad kiigaay dang gwii t'alang sdiihlda — the Giving Back the Name with Respect ceremony—Premier Campbell officially accepted the name, "Queen Charlotte Islands," returned to him. We placed the name in a traditional Haida bentwood box[4] and presented it to him in a joyous ceremony. Our people proudly wore traditional black, red, and white button blankets, cedar bark hats, headdresses with carved-mask frontlets, and sang, danced, and played the drums. The Premier presented the first school-globes with 'Haida Gwaii' labelled on our islands and gave them to Haida schoolchildren.

"And now everyone calls it Haida Gwaii—Islands of the People."

"Come here, my smart girl, I have something else to show you."

Grandfather took me to a small moss-covered hill, littered with tiny white specks. "Look."

I leaned over and reached down to pick up one of the pieces.

"No!" Grandfather shouted and it startled me.

I drew my hand back and quickly apologized.

"You mustn't disturb this. It's a shell midden, a place where the ancients discarded their shells and bones. Archaeologists will study it one day."

"But I want to study it now!"

Grandfather's eyes twinkled.

"I know the feeling. Sometimes we can find copper bracelets, ancient tools, and bones in these middens. I want to explore this as well, but the government forbids it. Come with me to the water's edge." He took my hand and led me to the shore. He pointed down at the water near the edge of the rocks and asked, "What do you see?"

I peered into crystal waters and saw nothing but transparent, button-sized jellyfish and a few fish swimming beneath them.

"There's not much to see here that we haven't already seen, Grandfather."

"Exactly!" he exclaimed as he pointed along the shore. "This is where your forefathers moved rocks from the deepest part of the shoreline, so they could slide their canoes ashore during low tide."

I closed my eyes and tried to picture them in their great canoes made of tall cedar trees. Grandfather had showed these great vessels to me at the Haida Heritage Centre at Kaay Llnagaay, Sea Lion Town, in Skidegate. I felt proud to know that my ancestors made such great vessels from cedar trees. We had depended on canoes for trade, for war, and for traveling from island to island, country to country. Grandfather interrupted my thoughts.

"And do you remember how we made our canoes, and how

34

ours were the most proficient of all?"

"Our canoes were as long as cedar trees are tall, and I remember the pictures you showed me and how some were small for hunting seal—"

"Those are eight meters or so," Grandfather interrupted me. He desperately wanted me to remember.

"Yes, Grandfather, and there were larger war-canoes, up to twenty-four meters long, which held thirty Haida."

"And how were they made?"

Grandfather liked to quiz me. I didn't mind.

"From one single trunk of a large cedar tree. They softened it with boiling water and steam and spread it open to make it about two to three meters wide. They decorated it by painting the front of it."

I thought about the paintings of my people, how they were made of large figures, outlined with thick black lines. Many of my friends who were not Haida could not tell what the figures were, but I knew the difference between a bear and a frog, a raven and an eagle. The black ovoid shapes were distinctive of our people. Where some people saw monsters, I saw familiar creatures.

"You have listened well, Jada. Now, tell me how we used to live."

"In longhouses set close together on the shore, within which lived thirty or forty people."

"Mostly in winter, Jada. During the other seasons, we moved about fishing and hunting, but we always came home to our families in our villages."

"And came together for potlatches?"

Grandfather frowned.

"Until they were banned, as were our totems."

"Banned? Why were they banned?"

I didn't understand. Potlatches were ceremonies our chiefs used to announce marriages, name babies, transfer titles and privileges, and mourn those who had died. We feasted and sang and danced. We recited our family history to keep it alive, gave away valuable gifts to enhance our statuses, and fellowshipped with our friends and families. What was wrong with that?

"In 1884, they jailed any Haida who attended a potlatch, so we held them in secret. Still, it remained a crime until 1954, and, if we were caught, they took everything we had and jailed us. Many of the things in museums that you see were stolen from us at a potlatch."

"But why?"

"They banned our totems because they thought we worshipped them. We did not. They banned our potlatches because they assumed we were wasteful. They wanted us to become more like them. Because of this, they felt justified in taking for themselves our gifts, our totems, and our precious copper shields."

Grandfather had shown me his great-grandfather's copper shield and reminded me he had once owned many more, but they had been taken by the government. Copper was the ultimate symbol of wealth among our people, and chiefs exchanged shields at potlatches and weddings. I knew it hurt Grandfather to never see the shields of his own grandfathers. I wished I could help him to heal.

"But tomorrow we go to a potlatch, Grandfather. We will feast on salmon, herring roe, on kelp, cod——"

"Halibut and tuna—and your grandmother's mushroom soup!" Grandfather rubbed his belly.

I ran toward the totems with my arms open wide.

"And I will wear the new button-blanket Grandmother is making, and we are erecting a totem in memory of a great chief. See? Things are better now, Grandfather; it has all been given back to us."

I stopped and ran toward him, breathless with happiness.

Grandfather sighed, "Not all, young Jada, but much more than my own grandfather had, that is true. Things are better for us now. At least we have our land, we have our beautiful islands, and we can live as true Haida again, if we choose. If only your mother…"

"Grandfather, she loves you. She does, and I do too."

We walked in silence back towards the Watchman's cabin, pausing again at the mouth of the cave where my forefathers once lived. I envisioned my family living there, and my ancestors living in my parents' apartment in Prince George. I took out my iPhone and snapped a picture to put on Facebook.

"Stand in front of the cave, Grandfather, and I'll take your picture. Pretend you're making a micro-blade."

Grandfather squatted down with two stones in his hand. I took his picture and he laughed.

"We better get back to our ship, Jada," he declared as he stood and put his hand on my shoulder. "And on the way, you can tell me a story."

"Which one?"

"I think I'd like to hear about that crazy man named Noah and his great canoe."

End Notes:

[1] Float plane: A floatplane (or pontoon plane) is a type of seaplane, with slender pontoons (known as "floats") mounted under the fuselage; only the floats of a floatplane normally come into contact with water, with the fuselage remaining above water.

[2] Sgang Gwaay is part of the Gwaii Haanas National Park Reserve, and also a United Nations Education and Scientific and Cultural Organization (UNESCO).

[3] Daily Press, June 17, 1862

[4] A bentwood box is made from one piece of wood that is steamed and bent. Originally, bentwood boxes were made to store important goods such as food, clothing, and even toys like miniature canoes. Today, many Northwest Coast Native artists make bentwood boxes to sell to art galleries or museums.

BJORN THE LUNDEHUND
1020 AD

This is the story my great-grandmother told my grandmother, who in turn whispered the saga to me on a dark, arctic night when the stars twinkled like ice crystals in the ebony sky. Colossal, glowing banners of brilliant, shimmering colours waved in the heavens and danced with the stars. You call them Aurora Borealis, or Northern Lights, but my master's father, Erik the Red, said the great splendour was his gods, Thor and Odin, making war in the heavens.

I was merely a wee pup when my grandmother told me the details of our past. I snuggled close to the soft protective coat of my mother, Frida, and curled into a fluffy ball. The wind blew cold and harsh as I looked toward the sea and watched thunderous waves crash against the rocky shores of Greenland. In the light of my master's fire, dark, rolling billows of the Labrador Sea sprayed thick, bulbous swells

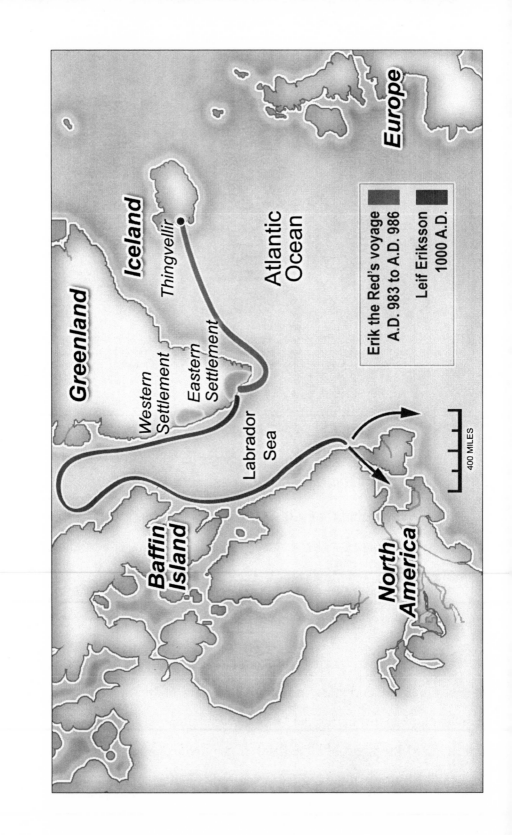

towards the sky and dispersed white fingers like comets.

I yawned and settled my fuzzy white chin on tiny paws. Grandmother, who was too old to move quickly, limped toward the fire, plopped down beside my mother and me, and rested her head on Mother's hip. She groaned as my master, Leif, passed by to stoke the fire he had left burning after fashioning a new sword.

"Are you okay, old Anja?" our master asked, as he scratched Grandmother's ears and patted her on the head. She grumbled and closed her eyes.

Leif loved my grandmother, and she was his constant friend and companion. She sailed many a dangerous voyage with Leif upon the indomitable, merciless seas.

I tilted my head to the side and spoke to Grandmother in high-pitched whines, "Grandmother, are you okay?"

Leif chuckled and scratched my head, too, "I haven't forgotten about you, little Bjorn. Go to sleep. It's a beautiful night."

He walked back to his long turf house with the grass roof and shut the door.

Grandmother sighed. "I'm fine, little Bjorn. Try to sleep. It's going to be a blustery, frosty night and you need your energy tomorrow when your mother teaches you to hunt puffins."

I pointed my nose to the sky and sniffed, "What are puffins?"

"Funny birds with bright orange beaks. Our Viking masters collect them for their meal tables, and we help them. If we succeed, we are given plenty of scraps to eat."

I popped my eyes open and stood, "I have seen those puffins, Grandmother! I can catch them, I know I can!"

My mother, Frida, pushed me down with a paw and licked my face, "See what you've done now, Mother? You've got him all wound up, and now he'll never sleep."

Grandmother grumbled, "Shhhh, little Bjorn. Your mother needs her rest too. Settle down now."

It wasn't easy trying to sleep. I knew if I was invited to hunt with my mother, it meant I was growing up. My eyes stayed wide open.

"Grandmother, can you tell me a story?"

"If you promise to go to sleep, I'll tell you a story."

"I want to hear the sagas."

"Where did you learn that word?" my mother laughed.

"I heard Leif tell young Snorre that a saga means 'what was said.' Tell me the sagas, Grandmother, from when you were born."

Grandmother sighed and licked my ears, "All right. Lie down and I will tell you all I can remember from what your great-grandmother told me. Settle in now."

I lay back down and snuggled into the crook of my mother's chest and counted the toes on her front paws. Six toes on each foot exactly like Grandmother and me. That's because we are Lundehunds and we all have six toes on each of our four paws. I didn't know other dogs only wore five.

Grandmother began her story and I listened carefully over the sounds of the waves. I drifted off to the land of Vikings and voyages on long ships.

Snuggle in, young reader, as I share the saga as Grandmother told it to me.

Long ago, when my master, Leif, was ten years old, my great-grandmother, Amma, was born.

"I want that one, *Föður!*"[1] Leif pointed to Amma squirming on the polar bear rug in the corner of the pit house where the thralls, Erik the Red's slaves, wove baskets and spun wool.

"She's a feisty one. She'll make a fine hunting dog and *matenot.*"[2] Erik lifted Amma off the rug and handed her to Leif who buried his nose in her fur.

"I'm going to show *Móðir!*"

Leif ran to the longhouse where his mother stood at a long hearth made of sturdy stone walls that stretched along the entire middle of the house. She stirred a stew of lamb and potato in a large iron cauldron with a
long metal rod.

"*Móðir!* Look what *Föður* gave me as a coming home present!"

"Awww, why now, isn't she fine? Let me see her toes. Does she have all six?" Leif's mother, Thorild, reached for Amma's paw, "One, two, three, four, five, six. Yes! All four paws, six each. Wonderful. Now, let me see her legs and neck."

---

1   Father in Icelandic

2   Companion in Old Norse

Leif handed Amma to his mother and she stretched out the puppy's front legs and swung her gently from side to side. The buffeting didn't hurt Amma because her joints were different from other animals. Thorild set the puppy down and stretched Amma's head up and backwards over her spine.

"Only a reindeer can do such a thing, Leif--other animals cannot reach their legs out side to side like this--and only the Lundehund and the reindeer can rest the back of their head on their shoulders."

"Why, *Móðir?*"

"So they can hunt *lundefugl*—puffins—on the screes. This way, they can walk slantways and up and down the rocks to catch them."

Thorild looked at the puppy's ears and laid them shut both backwards and forwards.

"What are you doing to her ears?"

"Making sure they close properly. Only Lundehund's ears can close. See? She lays them forward or backward to close them like so." Thorild showed Leif how the puppy could move her ears.

"Is she okay, *Móðir?*" Leif scrunched up his eyes in worry watching his mother's inspection.

"She's fine, very fine. You have a keen eye for picking a first-rate dog. What are you going to name her?"

"Amma."

"Ohhh, that means grandmother. Indeed, I think she will be a

44

good mother and grandmother. That's a wise choice for such a sweet girl. Remember, she will miss her mother tonight. Keep her with you so she's not afraid."

"Oh, don't worry, *Móðir,* I'll keep her with me always. I know what it's like to miss my mother too."

Leif scrunched his eyebrows remembering how he had been sent away at the age of eight, as is the custom for Viking boys. He lived with one of his father's slaves name Thryker, who taught him how to read and write runes and how to speak in the Celtic and Russian tongues. Thryker, who was a careful teacher, also taught Leif how to trade, use weapons, and use plants for food and medicine. Most important of all, he taught Leif how to recite sagas and poetry, which the Vikings loved as much as their families, food and ships.

Of all of his training, Leif's favourite lessons were those of the sea. When he wasn't studying with Thryker, he ran to the harbour with his friends to watch the ships come in. He'd listen to tales the sailors told of sea monsters and new lands full of trees and gold.

Now, Leif was 12 years old and considered a Viking man, but like all boys his age, he didn't mind that his mother still treated him as a little boy as long as no one else was watching.

"Can I have some lamb to feed Amma, *Móðir?*"

Thorild clucked her tongue, "Only if you give it to her in tiny pieces. She's not used to eating meat yet." Leif's mother picked a small bit of lamb from the cauldron and handed the tender morsel to him, "Careful now; it's hot."

The puppy's nose wiggled towards the mutton as Leif blew on the fresh scrap and smashed the fragrant meat with his fingers.

"Here you go, Amma," he giggled, as Amma licked every bit off his palm. "She loves it."

"Of course she loves it. She's a Viking dog."

"Thorild! Thorild!" Erik the Red stormed into the house, his dark blue eyes blazing with the fire of impatience.

"What now, Erik? Calm down."

"Where's the masthead I left here before I went to the green land?"

"Where you left it."

"Thorild!" Erik's face turned red, matching his red hair, "I want that mast!"

"Erik, remember your temper. We have another ninety days before we leave on our journey. Go to the pit house behind Hilde's house. It's still there under the walrus hide."

"I must have the mast if I'm going to be a chieftain in the green land. Come, Leif; I want to show it to you."

"Can I bring Amma?"

"Is she your *matenot*?"

Leif nodded.

"Then, of course, she must come."

Erik whistled, "Come, Gunnar!" His dog, Gunnar, the grandfather of Amma, ran to Erik's side. "Gunnar journeyed with me to the green land and back. A good Viking always keeps his dog with

46

him, and a good Viking dog always comes when it's called. You will need to train Amma to do the same. Lundehunds are stubborn dogs. Watch me with Gunnar and learn."

Leif and his father walked to Hilde's house to look in the pit house for the mast his father had left in Iceland when he was forced to leave the island. Erik the Red had always wrestled with a blazing temper, and, after killing a man and his slaves in a fit of rage, he was exiled from Iceland for three years as punishment.

Now he had returned after finding a green land. He wanted to take his family and friends there to make a new home.

"*Föður*, will I like living in this new green land? Will there be puffins for Amma to hunt?"

"There are all the animals we have here. The grass is green, and there are even more puffins for little Amma to hunt."

They reached the pit house and walked inside to find the mast, intricately carved into the shape of a dragon, exactly where Thorild said the relic would be.

"Did you make this *Föður?*"

Erik nodded, "I did. It took an entire winter."

"It's terribly fierce. Will this beast scare the sea monsters, do you think?"

"That is my hope, young one. Now, let's take this mighty behemoth to your brothers and cousins down on the ship so they can fasten it. The sooner we scare away the evil spirits the better."

The mast was bulky and heavy. Leif was tall and strong, but

still too small to carry the mast by himself. Erik's great arms, the size of trees, made the mast look small and light.

"Have you always lived in Iceland, *Föður?*"

His father looked down at Leif tenderly, cradling a sleeping Amma in his arms.

"No, our people lived in Scandinavia until your grandfather killed a man and was banished."

"He got in trouble like you did?"

"I'm afraid we aren't known for our patience. We are too much like Thor and strike when we are angry. It's our way. Don't let this curse be yours, Leif. I don't like my temper. I don't know how to control it. It's Thor's curse on my head."

Leif loved his father, no matter how many mistakes he'd made. He wanted to know more about from where he came. "What do people do in Scandinavia?"

"All the things we do here. They farm, make jewelry and weapons, and recite poetry.

"And sagas?"

"Especially sagas. That's how we know who we are."

"And they build ships?"

"Greatest ships on earth. You are too young to remember how the wind pushes us atop the great oceans and the men row with giant oars when the wind sleeps. Our people go where others only dream."

"What is your favourite, *Föður?*"

"What do you mean?"

"What is your favourite thing in life?"

Erik stopped walking and set down the mast. He stood in front of Leif and put his hands on his shoulders.

"You, my son. You are my favourite. My family–your mother, you, your brothers and your sister–are all that matter most to me in the world. This, too, is the Viking way. We love our families. We fight, conquer, and die for them. Always remember that."

Leif felt warm and safe under his father's big hands.

"Is grandfather coming with us to the new green land?"

"No, your grandfather, the great Thorvald Asvaldsson, will stay here in Hawsdale where he is a Chieftain."

Erik heaved the mast upon his massive shoulders.

"Let's hurry. We need to get the dragon head to the ship and get home to eat your mother's stew. Tonight we go to the Thingvellir."

"I've never been to the Thingvellir. I can hardly wait. What's it like?"

"It's a common-meeting and since you like stories, you will enjoy it. The lawman will recite the laws so we will remember them, and if the Thingvellir approves, you can carve our next journey on a rune stone."

⊗

After supper, Leif tucked Amma inside his tunic and, with his father and brothers, filed into the biggest longhouse in the village. Women and children weren't allowed at the Thingvellir. His sister

49

and mother stayed outside in the courtyard to gossip with other village women, while darning hosen and spinning wool. Children played tag, chased great auks and tried to guess what was happening behind the mysterious, closed doors of the Chieftain's longhouse.

Inside, Leif sat beside his father on a long bench nailed to the wall and held Amma gently inside his tunic. Men squeezed in side-by-side, eager to hear the village gossip and the sagas of Erik the Red. The room flickered with light from cod liver oil and cotton grass lamps, while the fire in the middle of the room kept them warm. Leif rubbed his hand on the sheep skin he sat upon and waited impatiently with the rest of the crowd for the Thingvellir to begin. Amma wiggled and snored inside his shirt, and he could feel her tiny breaths next to his skin. He smiled to himself, happy to have a *matenot* to call his own.

His grandfather, the Chieftain, motioned to the lawman who stood in the middle of the room beside the crackling fire. He recited the laws so loudly that Leif feared the daisies growing on the roof would uproot and join Odin and Thor in the sky. After the lawman finished, he pointed a burly hand at Leif's father and spoke in a commanding voice that vibrated on Leif's skin, making him shiver.

"Erik the Red."

The lawman stepped toward Erik and extended a fat, scarred finger.

"You were banished from Iceland for a period of three years because you killed a man in anger. You have returned for supplies and now wish to take people with you to a new land you claim to have found. Is this true?"

Leif trembled and held Amma closer as he looked at his father. He remembered how he had clung to his father's strong legs four years ago before he left. He was ashamed to cry, but he couldn't help it. He loved his father.

"Shhh, Leif. Be brave." His father picked him up and wiped his tears away, "I will come back for you as soon as I find good land for our farm. I promise."

Leif watched Erik stand before the Thingvellir and speak. He was glad Father came home so Leif could accompany him to the new green land.

"Dear countrymen, for four years I stayed far from these shores because I was banished. While on my journey, I discovered and sailed the coast of a magnificent green land. I explored its plenteous fjords and found no people living there. Enough land is to be had for any man to become chieftain of his own colony. There is plenty of grass to feed your livestock and good soil for growing crops. Enough animals live on these shores to make us fat: great white bears--much bigger than we've ever seen--foxes, hares, seals and walruses, puffins and other sea birds. When you put your foot on shore you step on dinner."

Everyone at the Thingvellir laughed, and Erik's red whiskers vibrated with the great force of his voice. He raised his hand and spoke again.

"In ninety days, I will take whoever wishes to go with me in their own ships. I have spoken."

Erik sat down beside Leif. In the new green land he would be a great Chieftain and no one could tell him what to do, but first, he needed the approval of the village and the blessing of his father.

The village men talked among themselves. Fertile land was becoming scarce by the sea in Iceland. The trees were almost all gone, and the over-grazed fields provided little food. If people left to start new colonies, there would be more room for their own farms. Leif watched his grandfather nod to the lawman.

The lawman spoke.

"Erik the Red, you may take as many people with you as can provide ship and supplies. We have spoken."

The coming days were filled with the sounds of hammers, building and repairing ships. Ironsmiths made tools and weapons for the Vikings to take with them to the new green land. Leif and Amma watched the artists carve intricate pictures into the edges of the great ships. Gigantic oars were hewn from enormous logs and the fierce dragon's head mast was placed on the prow of Erik the Red's knarr.[3]

Twenty-five ships would travel to the new green land. Leif watched the men ready the ships for the voyages and the women prepare food, make clothing, and pack supplies. When he wasn't learning to carve, Leif cared for his father's sheep, pigs and dogs.

Finally, the time came to board the supplies and animals for the great journey.

"C'mon, Amma! Help me with the sheep!"

---

3   A knarr is a Viking cargo ship built for Atlantic Ocean voyages.

Amma, ran beside Leif and barked. She followed her mother among the animals and tried to drive them to the ship.

"Föður!" Leif waved at his father and pointed to Amma.

Erik the Red threw back his head and laughed at the puppy trying to nip at the heels of his master's sheep.

"She learns fast! Just like her father!"

Leif ran from his father's farm to the ship with Amma close behind. Together they herded pigs, goats and cattle onto Erik's knarr and secured them in the middle of the vessel.

Leif's mother met him at the barnyard, her arms full of furs.

"Leif, when you're finished helping your father with his animals, I need your help gathering the cats."

"Yes, *Móðir.*"

Leif pushed a stubborn pig through the gate.

"How many do you have?"

"I'm not sure, but get as many as you can. They are good mousers, and we'll need them in the new green land as much as we do here."

Amma nipped at a pig's tail and barked. Leif's mother smiled. "You're growing up, Amma. Good girl!"

After Leif loaded all his father's animals, he headed toward the house to find a satchel for the cats. He'd only taken a few steps off the ship when he was knocked down by a young girl running with a basket of glass beads. Beautiful red, blue and yellow beads flew across the shipyard and into the mud and grass. The girl's eyes flashed with anger.

"Now look what you've done, you clumsy Viking!"

Amma barked at the girl and licked at Leif's face. Leif lay on the ground, looking up at a red-cheeked lass with eyes as blue as the Labrador Sea. The sun framed the back of her head, and her red braids sparkled. Leif had never seen such a pretty girl.

"I…I didn't mean to. I…"

"Get up this instant and help me collect these or my father will beat you and drag you to the Thingvellir where you will be exiled and live a long and lonely life on the sea."

Leif jumped up and laughed. "And who is your father?"

"None of your business."

Leif helped the girl gather the beads. "My name is Leif. What's yours?"

"It's of no concern to you."

"Oh, I see. And where were you going in such a hurry?"

"To my brother's knarr. He's going on a voyage to a new green land."

"I'm going too. I'm helping my father load the animals."

Leif poured the beads he collected into the basket the girl held. Viking women coveted beautiful glass beads, and the girl's mother made jewelery for trade in the village.

"Whose beads are these?" Leif recognized the delicate craftsmanship—too fine for a young girl.

"My mother's. She makes the best in the village." The girl worked to hide a smile. She was proud of her mother's skill.

54

"Your mother's beads are beautiful. My mother would love them."
Leif smiled.

The girl scowled and put her nose in the air.

"Thorgunna! What's taking you so long?" shouted her brother
from the side of a knarr two ships behind Erik the Red's.

"Coming, Fridleif!"

The girl whipped her skirt around, and stomped away.

"Leif! The cats!" his mother shouted from the cargo area of his
father's ship, where she was arranging a basket of dried cod and honey.

"Thorgunna," Leif whispered.

He couldn't hear Thorgunna murmur his name the same as he
repeated hers.

CB

Leif and Amma gathered the cats and kittens and delivered
them to his father's ship. He'd never seen pigs, cows and sheep on a
knarr before. Some ships carried only animals and cargo. Other ships
carried only people. Erik the Red's ship carried both. Mothers with
crying babies sat in the middle of great swaying boats, rocking their
infants and scolding toddlers. Children helped their fathers tend to the
noisy animals and clean their pens. Men and women hung their vast
array of battle shields along the ship's edge and strapped swords to
their sides. The strongest men and their thralls sat on trunks covered
in walrus skins to oar the boats when the wind would cease to blow
into the enormous rectangular sails.

After all the animals and people boarded, and they finally set out to sea, Leif held on to Amma to keep her from being trampled.

"Amma, look at all these people following my father to the new green land. He must be a great Chieftain for so many to trust him."

He stood on his toes on the ship's bow and looked for Thorgunna. He caught her looking in his direction from shore and thought he saw the faint hint of a smile. He watched Iceland grow smaller and smaller until he could no longer see his childhood home.

Leif jumped down to help his mother with the spices and wine. He rearranged the grain bins and carefully set his father's collection of carved ivory gods in between the wool and fur pallets, where he made a bed for Amma and himself. He loved the feeling of the cold sea spraying his hair and cheeks. Amma stood on her back legs and barked at the waves.

Erik the Red, standing at the stern of the ship and holding on to the ship's rudder, laughed, "She's scaring away the sea monsters. I knew she'd make a fine dog, a fine dog indeed."

"Have you ever seen a sea monster, *Föður?*"

Erik nodded his head and his eyes went dark and serious.

"Indeed I have. They are larger than this ship, with great tails and mouths that can swallow many vessels. May Thor and Odin keep them far from us."

Leif shivered and wrapped his fur cape closer. He licked the salty water from his lips and pushed his hair, wet from the briny ocean mist, from his face. Behind his father's ship sailed twenty-four ships bearing hopeful Chieftains looking for a new land to call home. He couldn't hear the babies cry anymore. The sea roared as loud as thunder and the waves grew taller than the dragon's head on the mast of his father's ship.

His father stood at the stern, gripping the rudder and looking at the sky for guidance. The animals grew strangely quiet and Amma sat beside Leif and looked up at him with her eyes full of questions.

"Don't worry, Amma. Father will get us there safely. There's nothing to fear of the sea monsters and waves."

Leif's stomach grumbled, and, as if his mother could hear it, she handed him a piece of dried cod and a glass of sour milk.

"Eat up. You'll need your strength."

At night Amma curled up with Leif in the bow under the watchful eye of the dragon mast. Leif enjoyed the motion of the sea and the way the rolling waves rocked him to sleep. His father still stood at the rudder, looking toward the sky for direction. His mother fell asleep holding her satchel of beloved cats.

When Leif awoke several hours later, he saw walruses float by on drifting ice. The icy isles clinked like glass and the wind bit at his cheeks and formed icicles on his eyebrows. His mother scurried among the ship's animals and worked her way to Leif with more sour milk and dried fish.

"Leif! Thorild! Get down with the animals. A storm comes! Quickly, thralls, down with the sail!"

Leif didn't want to hide with the animals. He wanted to help the thralls bring down the sail and help his father steer the ship. Before he could protest his mother grabbed his cape and pulled him to sit with her among the cows and sheep. Leif looked behind him and saw the angry sea toss the great vessels that followed like tiny marbles skipping along a pond. He craned his neck to see if Thorgunna's brothers were safe, but the rolling waves stood too tall.

Someone's cow fell overboard and went floating by along with someone's pack of furs. A cat sat atop a floating basket, soaked and scared. Leif reached for the frightened creature, but his mother pulled him back in beside her.

"Don't be foolish, Leif. We skin cats for gloves. There's nothing to be done. The sea is greedy and will take all it wants. The gods are angry and will swallow you too, if you let them."

Leif and his mother moved to where sheep lay bleating. Frightened cattle stomped their feet, and Amma barked and pulled on Leif's shoe straps. Waves slapped at Leif's face, and his mother's jars of honey rolled along the floor. His mother pulled him down to the floor of the ship and covered Amma and him with the giant fur pelt of a polar bear. Inside the pelt the air was warm and dry.

Leif looked at his mother and wiped the sea out of his eyes with the tail of his tunic.

"Will the sea be angry for long?"

"I hope not."

"Is *Föður* safe?"

"Your father is strong and experienced. This sea is no match for him."

"I should be with him, *Móðir*, not with you, hiding under a pelt." She nodded.

""Tis true, but this is the worst storm I've ever seen. I don't think the gods will mind you staying here where it's safe. The next storm will be your chance to fight. For now, be thankful to settle here and keep your *Móðir* warm."

Leif and his mother slept soundly under the protection of the fur pelt, where the thick skin and waterproof fur blocked out the thunder and the angry billows of the sea. Soon, they were warm and even Amma drifted into dreams of chasing puffins in the new green land.

When they awoke, Leif looked behind him and counted only thirteen ships. The others were lost at sea or turned back to Iceland. The ships directly behind his father no longer contained as many livestock. He knew that sadly, the ravenous sea had devoured them.

Leif's father pointed toward the front of the ship.

"Leif! Ahead!"

Leif looked toward the bow and saw a great wall of rock. The ship sailed in between two giant stone walls, weaved in and out of towering ice bergs, and sailed into a deep fjord.

"Are we home, *Föður?*"

"We're home! Oh yes, we're *home*," Erik the Red's voice echoed off the walls of the fjord, and Amma and Gunnar barked in excitement.

As soon as the ship pulled into shore, Leif put out the plank and with Amma led the animals off the ship. Everywhere Leif put his feet, green grass softened his steps, exactly as his father had described. Soon, all the ships pulled into the fjord, but did not stay. They sailed on to other fjords to claim their own lands.

 CB

It was a happy life in Greenland where Leif learned to hunt polar bear dressed in skins while floating on ice. He made bear cubs his pets, and Amma and he played by the roaring fires inside the long house. Amma bore a litter of puppies every year, and Leif traded them for the glass beads and medallions his mother loved to wear.

Visitors didn't come often, but one day an explorer named Bjarni Hergelson came to sit at his father's table. He told stories about a new land thick with trees. He talked about a new king in Norway named Olav Trygvason, the greatest, strongest Viking alive.

"Did you walk on this new land?" Leif asked, as he popped a roasted potato in his mouth.

"No, I wanted to get to Greenland," Bjarni replied, as he ripped hunk of meat off the ham shank and tore the tender meat with his teeth. "I was hungry."

Leif scowled, and his eyebrows twitched in slants above his eyes. If he had seen such a land with trees, he would have stopped to get wood. There wasn't much wood in Greenland, and they needed wood for fuel and to build ships.

"Someday, I will visit the great king and see the new land and bring back trees," Leif announced with such certainty the hall grew quiet and everyone looked at their Chieftain, Erik the Red. Erik put down his cup, leaned forward, and looked his son in the eye. He leaned back and lifted the cup.

"To my son, Leif, who will bring back trees!"

"To Leif!" the Viking hall shouted and everyone laughed and saluted Leif, while Amma barked and chased her tail.

As Leif grew older, so did Amma, and one night, after a full day of chasing puffins and playing with her children and grandchildren, she went to sleep and never woke up. Leif was a man by that time and tried not to cry, but when he found himself alone in the fields, he allowed tears to fall. Amma had been a faithful friend, and he would miss her. Her daughter, Anja, sat beside him the whole day and tried to comfort him.

"We'll sure miss her, won't we, Anja?"

Anja licked Leif's face as he carved one of his father's gods, Thor, out of a walrus tusk. He would present the idol to Erik the Red at the Thingvellir and ask for permission to take his own ship on a grand voyage to meet the great king and discover the land with trees.

He laid down his tools and reached into the pouch he wore on his belt. He looked at the comb he'd made out of whale bone for his mother. He took out a second comb he'd made for himself and combed his hair. He needed to look good to speak at the Thingvellir. A good Viking was always well groomed.

At the Thingvellir, Erik the Red not only gave Leif permission to find the land with trees, but decided to travel along, first to Iceland and then to Norway. But during the busy days leading up to the voyage, Erik fell from his horse.

At the longhouse that night, Erik the Red gave Leif bad news.

"It's a bad omen that I fell from my horse on the eve of this journey. Leif, you will go yourself to Norway to meet this great king. Take him all the gifts I've put aside and speak to him only after his stomach is full."

Erik gave Leif his own ship and appointed Thryker and fourteen men to go with him. On his journey, his ship was blown off course and landed on the Island of Hebrides. After spending a month on the island, they set off again for Norway, where Leif could meet the great King Olaf and worship his father's gods at the temple.

When they arrived in Norway, Leif couldn't stop craning his neck, looking at the fine houses and beautiful wharves. But people stared at Leif too, as he walked through the streets with gifts for the king. Never before had they seen such a large polar bear cub. The wealth of furs and tusks Leif's men carried behind him made people stop in the streets and point in awe.

"Where is the temple of the gods?" Leif asked a merchant in the street who pulled Leif into an alley and put a finger over his lips.

"They are no more. King Olaf forbids them and tore them all down. We no longer worship our ancestor's gods. You must never be caught with idols. Shhh."

62

This puzzled Leif. Why wouldn't the king worship Thor and Odin as his father did?

When the king heard of a young man from Greenland who led white bears through the streets, he sent his warriors to bring him to his kingdom.

"But I must first fix my hair," Leif said. "I will see the king after his stomach is full."

After King Olaf ate his fill, Leif sent his gifts into the king's great hall. Anja whined.

"Shhh, little girl," Leif said, "Be patient as your mother was patient. We will see the king soon enough."

Other dogs sat under the king's table, licking up the scraps and bones their masters threw on the floor. The king's men drank from large bull's horns while women poured mead and refilled the tables with food. Leif felt eager to share his mother's mead with the king.

"Who brings me such fine gifts?" the King demanded as he looked down the dark hall to see who stood in his doorway. His blue eyes reflected the fire in the middle of the hall that burned to warm them. Leif entered with his polar bear and Anja at his side.

"It is I, Leif Eriksson, son of Erik the Red."

Would the king invite him in? Or would he remember how his father and grandfather were banished from the great land of Norway and forbid him?

"I knew your father! Come in! Come in!"

The King not only invited Leif in, but they became fast friends.

63

Because Leif appeared well-mannered and well-groomed, the King invited him to stay at his court for the winter.

One day while Leif and the King played chess, the King told Leif about how a man named Christ had defeated Odin and Thor and thrown them into the underworld.

The king moved a pawn forward on the chess board. "And that is why I destroyed all their temples."

"How did you do such a thing without the people rebelling?" Leif sought the answer as he moved his bishop on the chess board.

"I challenged them to contests. I asked them to pray to their gods and I prayed to mine, and then I out-swam, out-ran, and out-fought them in martial arts. I challenged them to archery contests and mortal combat. When I won, they knew that Christ is greater than Thor and Odin and all their other gods."

"If the great Odin and Thor can be defeated by this great God-Christ you speak of, then I must worship Him, too, and make sacrifices as my father instructed me."

The king shook his head.

"There are no sacrifices but love for this God. He is the One True God. His sacrifice on the cross paid for all sacrifices."

Leif learned more about Christ, threw away his father's idols, and followed King Olaf's God by being baptized.

Soon the time came to journey home to Greenland. King Olaf gave Leif two slaves named Haig and Haigie. A priest and other holy men also traveled with Leif on his voyage so that they could help tell the people of Greenland all about the God who conquered Odin and Thor.

On his way home, during a terrible storm that nearly tossed Anja overboard, Leif's ship lost its way. The morning after the storm, Leif woke up and saw a land full of trees. He sailed along the border until he found a shallow bay.

"Look, Anja!"

Leif and his men disembarked and marveled at this new land. Streams glistened with salmon and the forests overflowed with trees so tall Anja couldn't see the tips of them. Anja rolled on the thick green grass and took a drink from a clear cold stream where tiny fish jumped and crabs scuttled past her nose.

"Woof!" Anja barked, wagging her tail and running circles around Leif. Leif picked up a stick and threw it, and Anja bounded across a meadow full of butterflies, hares and red foxes.

Leif and his men plucked blueberries and damsons and gathered cherries, raspberries and partridge berries to take home. Cranberries, cloudberries and squashberries grew in abundance. Everywhere they looked there was plenty to eat and plenty of trees for wood to make ships and use for fuel.

"Leif! Over here! Look! Grapes!"

In one section of the forest, wild grapes grew in clinging vines all over the floor in between and along the trunks of birch trees.

"Eat to your fill, men. Enjoy the fruit of your voyage!"

That night around a warm fire, Anja's belly bulged as she lay on her side panting beside Leif.

"Anja, I think you ate one too many rabbits." Leif laughed and scratched her ears. "That's okay. You have plenty of time to rest. We will stay here for the winter to gather supplies and build. Then, we'll go to Greenland in the spring to bring families back to live on this new land I will now call Vinland, for the many vines of fruit we find here."

Anja didn't know it, but Leif and his men were the first Europeans to find this land and live on it. They spent the winter building turf houses and chopping trees to take back to Greenland to build ships.

In the fall, after Anja bore a litter of puppies, Leif bent down to where Anja hid under a longhouse cot with her brood.

"Good girl, Anja. They are beautiful babies: two boys and a girl. How fine. We will keep the little girl and name her Frida."

Anja licked Leif's hand and pushed her babies close to her with her nose. They were the first Lundehunds born in the new land.

In the spring Leif and part of his crew, along with Anja and the puppies, sailed home to Greenland. Their ship lay deep in the water, bulging with fruit, lumber and the livestock that were born in Vinand. Leif looked proudly at the baskets full of grapevines he'd packed to take with them.

On their journey home, Leif's keen eyesight noticed something strange on the horizon. His crew didn't understand why he steered so close to shore.

"What are you doing, Leif?"

"Don't you see that unusual formation ahead?"

No, they couldn't see it. Leif's eyesight was much better than theirs.

When he got closer, everyone could see people stranded on a reef. Leif invited the fifteen people aboard his ship and took them safely with him home to Eriksfjord, Greenland.

Everyone in Greenland celebrated his return.

"I feared the sea monsters got you, brother!" His sister, Freydis, cried as she hugged him and helped carry the baskets of fruit to her father's house. "You are so lucky, Leif, to find such bounty!" People of the village began to call him "Leif the Lucky."

"That makes you lucky dogs, too, Anja and Frida." Leif laughed, and Anja barked, happy to be home with her friends. Frida stumbled behind Leif, learning for the first time how it felt to be home in Greenland.

That night as everyone sat around the fire, their stomachs full of the fruit and meat Leif had brought them, he told them about the One True God.

"This God. He is greater than Thor and Odin. He captured them and threw them into the underworld. He is the God of Norway now."

"That cannot be!" Erik the Red's eyes blazed, "I will not hear it." He stomped out into the darkness to watch the Northern Lights. Leif turned toward his mother.

"It is true, *Móðir.* In Norway I gave my heart to this God and was baptized."

"Tell me more about this God that conquered the gods of your father. I want to know why you chose to worship Him."

"Christ was born to die as a sacrifice for our sins. He took all of our punishment. He is a healer and is compassionate and kind."

Leif's mother tilted her head and looked at Leif with a wrinkled brow.

"But how can someone kind be strong enough to defeat Odin and Thor?"

"Because He alone is the One True God. He makes blind eyes see and the lame walk. Thor and Odin never do that. And when King Olaf prays, The One True God answers his prayers and helps him win in battle. He destroyed all the idols in Norway and nothing bad happened to him. The idols were nothing more than rotted wood where rats lived, eating offerings left by frightened Vikings. This Christ-God—He doesn't threaten us. He loves us. He hears us when we pray."

Leif's mother grasped her son's strong hands.

"I, too, want to follow this God of whom you speak. I want to know a God Who hears prayers and gives such love."

Leif and the priest that traveled with him shared the good news of Christ with everyone in the village. Many came to be baptized, including Leif's mother. She built a little church inside a circular courtyard and spent much of the rest of her life praying and worshipping God, along with other converts.

Erik the Red refused to worship the One True God. He refused to visit the little church.

Soon after Leif's return, families gathered supplies to prepare for a move to Vinland. His brother Thorvald took thirty people with him on the voyage to make a colony in Vinland and explore more. They loved their life in Vinland, where the land provided plenty of food and water for them and their livestock. They built houses out of stones, turf, and wood and stored food for journeys and trade. That first winter a baby boy named Snorre was born. He was the first European born in North America.

One day, when Snorre toddled about in the meadow chasing a muskrat, dark-skinned people in canoes arrived at the settlement and pulled their boats ashore. The Vikings called these people *Skraelings*. For several months the *Skraelings* traded with the Vikings and ate with them.

But one day, hundreds of *Skraelings* arrived on the shores and attacked the Vikings. The Vikings fought back and scared the *Skraelings* away, but after the invasion, the Vikings decided Vinland no longer provided a safe place to raise their children, and they sailed back to Greenland, never to return to that part of the world in their generation.

ଔ

My grandmother finished the saga and fell asleep. I yawned, stretched and listened to Snorre giggle in Leif Eriksson's longhouse. Tomorrow Snorre would become my master. I knew this because I heard Leif tell him earlier that day.

Tomorrow I would also hunt puffins. Strong and agile, I would make my grandmother proud. I was a Viking dog, my master's *matenot.* I would be faithful the way my grandmother and mother were faithful to Leif Eriksson: the first European to discover the land people would one day call Canada.

Photo: Wikimedia / Public Domain / taken by Karen Elise, Norway 2003

A Letter from the Author:

Dear Reader,

Bjorn didn't know people would one day call the place where the Vikings settled, L'Anse Aux Meadows, Newfoundland, Canada. He couldn't know his breed of dog would dwindle down to a mere six Lundehunds in 1963.

In 2008 the American Kennel Club recognized the Norwegian Lundehund as an official breed. On January 1, 2011, the Norwegian Lundhund received full AKC recognition.

Lundehunds are funny little dogs with big personalities. They are stubborn, intelligent, and curious. They are a primitive breed and therefore share the habits of foxes and wolves. They like to hide their food around the house, tunnel into tiny spaces, and climb onto countertops. They are hard to train because they are stubborn like a cat and have minds of their own. They are independent and strong-willed, much like the Vikings who once made these delightful little dogs their beloved matenots.

Of all the Viking dog breeds, the Norwegian Lundehund is the most ancient. One Lundehund could capture 30 puffins in one night, a delicacy for Vikings. At one point, the Lundehund was as valuable as a milk cow. Vikings could own anywhere from one or two dogs to a pack of two dozen.

When archaeologists find a Viking grave, they usually find a dog buried with their master. Vikings not only owned dogs to help them herd animals, but they were also a Viking's companion and very best friend.

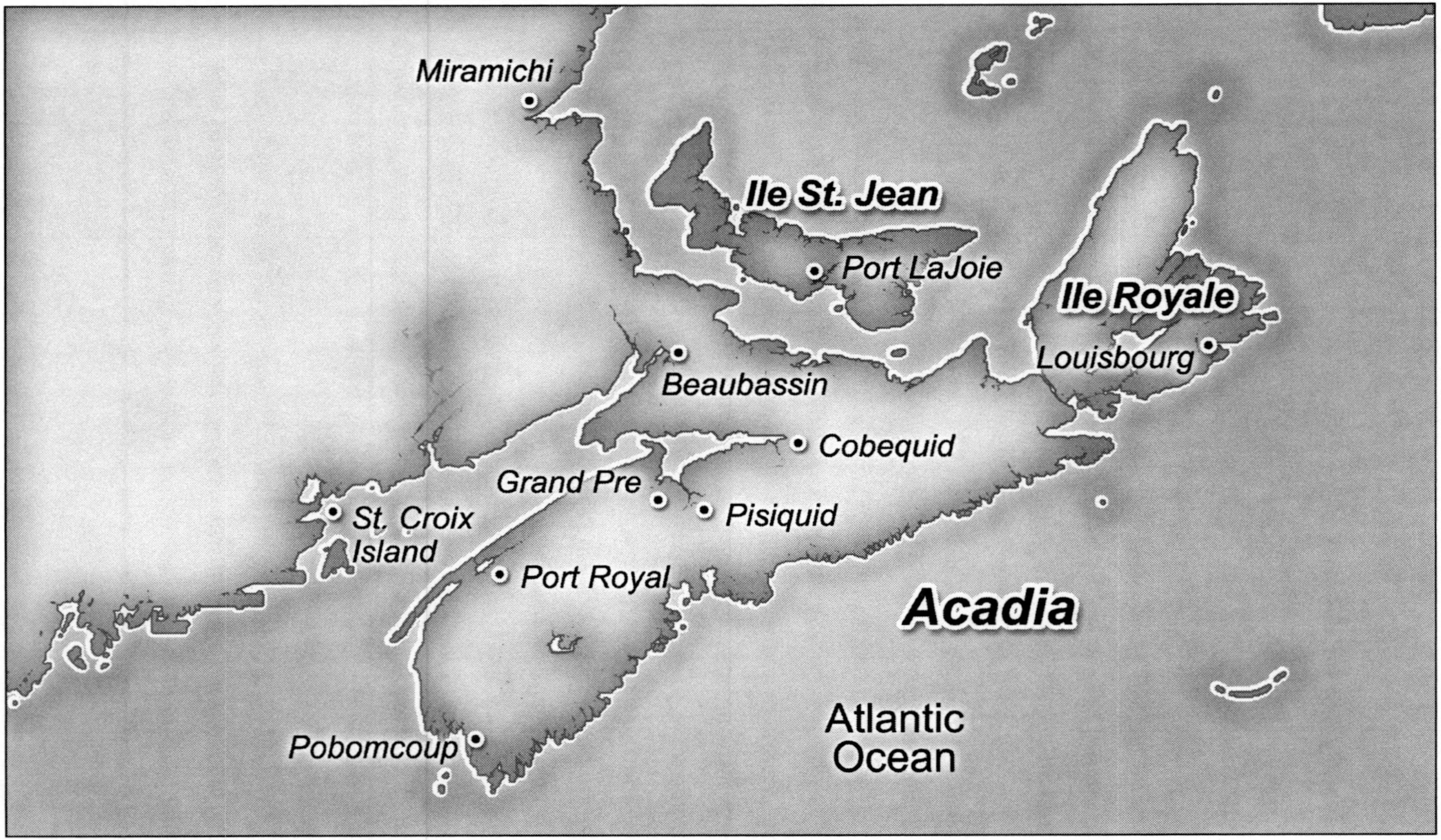

Ile Royale

Louisbourg

Ile St. Jean

Port LaJoie

Acadia

Cobequid

Beaubassin

Pisiquid

Atlantic
Ocean

Grand Pre

Port Royal

Miramichi

St. Croix
Island

Pobomcoup

THE OLD VIOLIN
1755

"Hark! how those lips still repeat the prayer, 'O Father, forgive them!'

Let us repeat that prayer in the hour when the wicked assail us,

Let us repeat it now, and say, 'O Father, forgive them!'"

--Henry Wadsworth Longfellow, Evangeline

August 28, 2005 - New Orleans, Louisiana

"How much longer, *Pépé*?

Eleven-year-old Beaux Thibodeaux shivered as he balanced his sister on his back and slogged through chest high water in the streets of New Orleans. Ahead of him his grandparents fought their way through the murky stream where once there was dancing and music. Was it only yesterday the echoes of jazz musicians and people laughing filled the boulevards?

Today, rivers as high as stop signs flowed through alleys and corridors. No carriages with decorated horses ambled through the avenues with happy couples singing. The homes of Beaux's ancestors were under water, and now his family searched for a place of rescue.

Beaux's grandfather held a bundle of clothes over his head.

"Be careful, Beaux, and mind your step now, ya hear? This street chock a block wid junk. Ga! Here come Joe Landry wif da pirogue dere."

"*Mémé,* ma head hurts."

Beaux's little sister, Marie, fell ill the same time the hurricane's angry waves seized the levee of New Orleans and smashed it like a Louisiana mosquito.

"Shhh, *petite fille*, little girl. We're almost there," *Mémé* huffed, and Beaux worried that she and his grandfather would fall in the water that grew deeper with each step. How would he save them and his sister too?

Joe Landry rowed his pirogue toward the stranded family, and Beaux gently placed Marie in Joe's enormous brown tree trunk arms. Then he remembered.

"*Pépé! Ma violon!* I must go back!"

"*Non, non, ma cherie*, you cannot!" his Grandmother shouted above the sound of the water.

74

"But I must. Mother told me never to forget it."

"Leave it, Beaux. Let the pleece get it."

Grandfather helped *Mémé* into the pirogue.

Police? Beaux's Cajun *pépé* was crazy. Beaux couldn't see any police. People were breaking into houses not their own, looking for food and blankets, maybe even things to steal. He had to go back for the violin.

"Don't worry, *Pépé*. You can send someone to fetch me."

Beaux swam toward the house.

His grandmother cried out, "Oh, Beaux, *ma chère,* be careful!"

He could barely hear her over the driving rain and the cries of others looking for a way out of the flooded city. The tops of cars peeked out of the chest high water. Hurricane Katrina was not a genteel southern lady. She swallowed up roads, swept through dwellings, and had Beaux dog paddling back to his grandparent's house to retrieve his mother's old violin.

The water grew deeper. Beaux wondered if the father he had never met swam somewhere in the same flooded waters. He blocked the thought out of his mind and tried to picture the last time he heard his mother play her favorite songs. She could imitate all the sounds of the bayou and recreate the sounds of the city on the worn fiddle. She played the songs her father and grandfather had taught her from the old country. Before she died of cancer, she gave the violin to Beaux.

"This beautiful violin is in your hands now, Beaux. She's a priceless, treasured instrument handed down in our family, from old

France and Nova Scotia. Its soul has felt a lot of heartache and just as much happiness. Now you must help it resonate with its ancient stories."

She placed the treasured heirloom in his hands and he slept with it that night, not knowing that two weeks later she would die. She never told him how sick she was, and he was too young to understand.

Now the violin was his closest friend. When he placed the precious fiddle under his chin, he could still smell the scent of his mother in the aged wood and feel the indentation where her thumb had worn down the bow. When he played, he imagined her smiling at him, counting off measures, telling him which licks to play. That violin was the only thing he had left of her. He had to have it.

He swam to the edge of his grandfather's house and stood on the roof where he was eye to eye with the tops of telephone poles and the giant bulb of the light post that nightly shone into his bedroom and kept him awake. He wiped the rain out of his eyes and tried to dry his cold, trembling hands on the inside of his coat. He fought with the attic window until it gave way and let him inside the house that smelled of mold and *Mémé's* fried catfish and shrimp jambalaya.

When the storm had started, and *Pépé* spotted Percy Benoit's French bull dog, Adolphus, floating down the street atop Nadine Benoit's favorite couch, *Mémé* decided it was time to start moving things upstairs. Beaux helped his grandparents transfer all the most treasured things to the second floor of the house.

"Shouldn't we evacuate, like the mayor said on the news?"

Beaux asked his grandpa.

"Nah. I seen a million deze hurricanes. I ride 'em out before. I ride it out agin."

Pépé handed Beaux his grandmother's scrapbooks.

"*Pépé,* you a stubborn ol' fool."

Mémé shook her head and shuffled back to the kitchen to stir the jambalaya.

Now, for the first time Beaux could remember, his grandfather was wrong. Katrina wasn't any ol' hurricane. She raged furious and poured her relentless wrath against the fragile levees of New Orleans. The barriers collapsed and the ocean waters of the Gulf of Mexico burst into the city like an uninvited guest, while Katrina left a path of destruction over 93,000 square miles.

There was no electricity now, and with the sun sleeping behind rain clouds, Beaux could barely see while in the house. He walked down the attic steps to the second floor and peered over the loft railing. Black, murky water lapped across the chair where his grandmother sat every night knitting blankets for the church raffle. Beaux could hear the windows creak and felt the house sway from the force of the water lapping against the walls.

He went to his grandfather's room and found the violin in its wooden case on the top shelf of the closet, the same as it had been when his mother gave it to him.

"I found you, my beautiful *violon.*"

Beaux hugged the fiddle[1] close to his chest and went to fetch a white sheet. He climbed back onto the roof and tied the white sail to a lightning rod on top of the house. He crawled back inside and into his grandfather's bed without removing his wet boots. Soon, someone would see his white flag and come to get him. In the meantime he would sleep. Exhausted, he locked the *violon* in his arms and closed his eyes. He pictured the story his mother told him of the old *violon's* sad journey to Louisiana.

" *Vous devez toujours vous rappeler, ma chère, la grande déportation.* You must always remember, my dear, the Great Deportation. This *violon,* it has seen the tears of *nos ancêtres*—our ancestors. It must never, ever leave us."

August 1755

Belina yawned and felt underneath Henrietta's soft, feathery belly for an egg.

"Move, girl, you know what I've come to do."

The cranky hen responded with a throaty cluck. Belina patted the irritable chicken and moved quickly from nesting box to nesting box, breathing a sigh of relief each time her hand fell upon an egg and not a snake. She shuddered, remembering the snake she'd found while gathering eggs last summer. She'd refused to collect the eggs for days until her brother teased her so badly she had to prove her bravery. Finally, Jean-Baptiste confessed to Mama that he had placed the snake there. There were no snakes in Acadia that ate chicken eggs. Only small snakes that lived in the grass.

With her basket full of eggs, she latched the hen yard shut and hurried to the kitchen to show her mother the generosity of the hens. The rooster crowed in triumph, believing he had driven the intruder from his brood.

The little thatched-roof cabin, with its thick wooden door and mud-daub walls, was the only home Belina had ever known. She'd been born in the same room that currently housed the new hutch Papa made for Mama's kitchen things. Now the cabin had three rooms—the kitchen, a loft for Belina and her brother, and a tiny little room big enough for a bed for Mama and Papa.

"Look, Mama, we have enough for a quiche. Mama?"

Belina scanned the cabin and noticed the fire had gone out in the hearth. She picked up a root basket and headed to the garden to dig up turnips and potatoes. On her way she spotted her mother at the side of the house, building a fire in front of the outdoor oven that jutted out under a lean-to from the side of the house.

"There you are, Belina." Mama stood and wiped sweat from her brow. "You took longer to get the eggs."

"Yes, Mama. Henrietta seemed irritable, but she and the girls gave us enough eggs this morning for a quiche. Where is Papa and Jean-Baptiste?"

"Your brother is helping Madame Benoit pick apples and your father is helping Monsieur Bertrand build the dike for his new farm."

Belina giggled, remembering last week's wedding. Papa played his fiddle at the dance. The entire community helped build

Monsieur and Madam Bertrand's new house. It was the Acadian way.

"Why are you out here, Mama?"

"Don't you remember? Today we make candles for the winter. Hurry up with the turnips and potatoes so you can help me. But first, after the garden, take *dîner* to your father and Monsieur Bertrand."

"Yes, Mama."

Belina grabbed the fork hoe leaning against the house, skipped to the garden, and kicked off her wooden shoes. The soil was rich and fertile, the best land in North America. Belina was a robust, healthy girl because there was plenty of food for her family and the animals they raised. She had never been seriously ill with diseases such as scurvy, typhus, or cholera that afflicted colonists farther south. There was always plenty of fruit, vegetables and milk. She dug her hoe into the rich earth and imagined a smile on her father's face when she surprised him with tonight's *souper.*[2]

Back in the cabin, she set the basket on the thick wooden table her father made and set to work, gathering the food for his *dîner.* She pulled a clean basket off the hutch and lined it with a red and white linen towel. Her swift hands unwrapped a loaf of bread tucked safely inside one of Mama's wool napkins. Belina made the loaf yesterday morning, and it still smelled fresh and sweet. She cut two thick slices and spread them with butter and lard. To the basket she added salted pork, dried cod, cheese, and apples. She ran to the cool stream that flowed behind the barn and pulled out a bucket filled with a pitcher of this morning's milk and a crock of cold lobster caught yesterday by

80

Jean-Baptiste. She skipped back to the house and tucked them into the basket beside a small crock of bread pudding. Belina placed the heavy basket in a little wooden cart and pushed it to the marsh where her father worked in the blazing sun beside Monsieur Bertrand.

After she'd gone a mile she could see her father and his friend working on the dike they were building along the outer marsh area of Bertrand's farm. It was difficult work, but the result would be fertile soil for an abundance of crops. Other men had already helped drive six rows of logs into the ground. Now, Bertrand and Papa were laying logs one on top of another between the rows and filling all the spaces in between with packed clay. After that, the men would cover all of it with sod from the marsh.

Belina's favorite part of the dike was the *aboiteau*, a little one-way door in the dike that allowed fresh water to run off the marshes at low tide, yet kept the sea water out when the tide rose. This kept the salt off the farmland, making it extremely fertile. It would take four years for the snow and rain to wash away the salt from the marshes, creating the rich soil Bertrand and his bride needed to grow bountiful crops.

Everyone in Acadia worked together to keep the dikes repaired because they were all interconnected. If someone's dike broke, it flooded their neighbour's farmland. The Acadians were good neighbours.

"Bonjour, Papa!"

Belina rolled her cart to a nearby tree and spread an old quilt on the ground.

"Bonjour, Belina!"

Papa threw down a log and trotted over to where Belina unpacked the lunch.

"Papa, *avez-vous faim?"*

"Oui, I am hungry–thirsty too."

"I have brought you fresh milk and cream–cold. I put it in the stream this morning just for you."

"Merci."

Francois Thibodeaux leaned over the basket and sniffed.

"Ah. I smell your mother's bread pudding."

"I'm making *tarte aux navets et pommes de terre* for *souper,* Papa."

Francois eyes grew large.

"Non. Non. Non tarte aux navets et pommes de terre pour le souper!"

"Papa, you're teasing. You love turnip and potato pie."

Francois laughed.

"I love to tease *ma belle fille."*

Belina blushed as she did every time her father called her his beautiful girl in front of another. She motioned to Papa's friend.

"Will you join us, Monsieur Bertrand?"

"Non. Madame Bertrand is making my lunch. *Au revoir."*

The newlywed headed toward home.

"Au revoir."

Belina and her father waved as Bertrand headed up the hill to his new bride. Francois smiled and bit off a mouthful of bread.

Belina sliced some cheese and handed it to him.

"Will you dance with me tonight, Papa? After the dishes are put away?"

Francois sat on the blanket, leaned on the cart, and took a long drink of milk.

"*Oui, ma chérie,* it will be my pleasure to dance with you."

"Then I must hurry back to help mother and begin peeling the potatoes. You can bring the cart home at supper time."

Belina kicked off her wooden shoes and ran toward home.

"*Au revoir,* Papa!"

"*Au revoir,* Belina!"

Belina ran down the path toward home, but decided to take a shortcut past the stream behind the farm where she could cool her hot feet. Too soon the snow would fall and she would have to always wear shoes.

On a little rock rested a tiny Pickerel frog. Jean-Baptiste would like to see him. Belina forgot all about the turnips and potatoes waiting for her at home and chased the little frog down the stream. Carefully, she crept toward him and lunged. She fell on her stomach and came face to face with a large black boot.

She followed the line of the boot upwards and saw it attached to a scowling man dressed in a red coat.

"*Excusez-moi!*"

Belina jumped up, brushed off the front of her apron, and

straightened her bonnet. She had traveled farther down the stream than she realized and was standing in the churchyard a mile past her house. She'd never seen a man dressed this way before. She looked around at the tents pitched in the churchyard and finally found the friendly face of her priest, Father Landry.

The priest approached the soldier and motioned to Belina.

"She is a child at play, on her way home to her family–yes, Belina?"

Belina nodded. Father Landry's eye twitched, and he smiled stiffly at her. Why did he need to explain her actions to this soldier?

"Yes, Father Landry, *au revoir.*"

Belina ran home as fast as her legs would carry. Not only did she need to help mother, but her milk cow, Nicole, would be waiting to be fed along with the other animals on the farm, and she still needed to grate the potatoes and turnips for the pie she had promised her father.

"Mama! Mama!"

"What is it, *ma chérie?*

Madame Thibodeaux dipped wicks into the hot tallow.

"Mama, there are men in red coats living in tents in the churchyard."

"*Oui*. Madame Richard told me about them. They came on the ships docked on the river near the Minas Basin."

"Ships? May I go see them, Mama?"

"Belina, I need your help, and there is still *souper.* Perhaps tomorrow."

84

"Yes, Mama."

Belina helped her Mama but she couldn't stop thinking about those ships docked a short distance from her door. She loved to watch them, bigger than a barn, sliding across the water like a large house on ice. Mesmerized by the way they rocked gently back and forth, she thought it would be lovely to sleep on them for just one night. Father Landry had journeyed on a ship. She would ask him again what it was like to cross the great ocean from France and arrive here on the shores of Grand-Pré.

Mama had made most of the candles by the time Belina arrived home. Usually Jean-Baptiste and Belina made the candles, but Mama said Belina was too antsy to stand at the cauldron dipping wicks over and over again and gave her adventurous daughter other jobs that kept her feet and hands busy. The night before, Jean-Baptiste and Belina twisted strips of cloth into wicks and now Mama's candles hung from a rod beside the outdoor oven to cool and harden.

Belina helped Mama clean up the cauldron, start a fire in the outdoor oven, and fetch four buckets of water for the evening. Without sitting down to rest, she fed the animals and set to work making Papa's pie. She grated the potatoes and turnips and squeezed the water out of them with a cheese cloth, before adding salt pork and herbs. She thought about the angry soldier she'd seen and wanted to know more about him. She would ask Mama if she could invite Father Landry to *souper.* He loved to talk and would answer all her questions.

Mama entered the kitchen with her apron full of string beans.

She poured them into a bucket, heaved a deep sigh, and wiped her brow. Madame Thibodeaux was feeling more tired than usual. She smiled to herself, thinking of the news she would share with her children that evening. There would be joy in the house tonight.

"Mama, are you okay? You don't look well."

Belina grabbed a rag, dunked it in the cold stream water and placed the cool cloth on her mother's forehead."

"I'm fine, only a bit tired."

"You stood too long in the sun without your bonnet again, Mama."

Mama smiled. Even as a young girl she didn't like her bonnet.

"You are a good daughter, *ma chérie*. You will make a good mother and wife one day."

Belina carried the turnip and potato pie to the outdoor oven and, while it baked, made biscuits and a wild blueberry torte—Jean-Baptiste's favorite.

"I didn't know we had berries, Belina."

Mama sat at the table snapping beans.

"I've been saving them for a surprise. I picked them yesterday when I was playing with Pierre."

"You are getting too old to play with Pierre alone. Where was Veronique?"

"She was with us, but Pierre and I went hunting for rabbits while Veronique made cattail baskets. That's when I found the berries."

86

"From now on, you must not be with Pierre alone in the woods. It's not proper."

"Pierre is like a brother, Mama. We've grown up together."

"Yes, I know. But you are becoming a young lady, and Pierre a young man."

"Can we invite Father Landry to supper, Mama?"

"Oui. I have some questions I want to ask him. I imagine you do too?"

Mama raised her eyes at Belina who shrugged. Mama smiled and reached across the table for a berry and plopped the juicy fruit in her mouth.

"Your papa and brother will love those. Tomorrow you can gather more blueberries and I will make *tartes* for Widow Rimbaut and one for Father Landry—whom you better fetch because, from the smell coming out of the oven, it is nearly time for *souper.* Run along and I will put the torte and biscuits in to bake."

Belina blew Mama a kiss, plopped her bonnet on her head and ran down the lane toward the church. She cut through the woods and emerged onto the road where she met Father Landry.

"Belina! What are you doing roaming in the woods alone this time of year? The moose are thick these days."

"I'm not afraid of a moose, Father. You're silly."

"Remember White Owl? He was blessed that the moose only stepped on his foot and broke it."

"How is his foot now?"

"White Owl's? Or that of the Moose?" Father Landry teased.

"White Owl, Father," Belina giggled.

"Much better. He went hunting today, which is why I know the moose are running scared."

Belina laughed at the thought of all the forest's moose running away from White Owl.

"Father Landry, my Mama would like you to join us for *souper.*"

"My pleasure, Belina. I was on my way to see your papa."

"He will be home soon. I've made turnip and potato pie!"

"Are you old enough, Belina, to make turnip and potato pie? I remember christening you yesterday."

"Father, I'm twelve now!"

"Twelve already? Have you a beau?"

Father Landry's eyes twinkled with mischief.

"Father, I will never marry. I want to stay with Mama and Papa and be their daughter forever."

"You could join the sisters" smiled Father Landry.

Belina skipped along beside him.

"I could never be that devout, Father. I like to chase frogs and climb trees. And sometimes, I have wrong thoughts."

"Do you need a confession?"

"Not yet. But I know I will need one soon. I know how I am. Can we do a pre-confession?"

Father Landry threw back his head and laughed.

"*Non, ma chérie,* there is no pre-confession in the church. But it is delightful that you are concerned. You are a good Catholic girl."

Belina pointed toward the house.

"Oh look! Papa's home! And Jean-Baptiste is carrying in the wood."

Jean-Baptiste waved at the priest and his sister, and Father Landry waved back. Belina ran toward her father to meet him and push the cart he'd brought home.

"Papa, Father Landry is joining us for *souper.* He has news for you. There are ships in the harbor, and Mama said maybe tomorrow I can go see them."

Monsieur Thibodeaux looked toward the priest who wore a grim and somber face. The priest shook his head at Father, but Belina didn't see. Papa looked down at his beaming daughter and smiled.

"Go inside, *ma chérie,* and prepare a grand feast, for you have two papas at your table tonight."

Belina bounced into the house and helped Mama set out earthenware plates and mugs and heaped a wooden bowl full of fruit in the middle of the table. This time of year yielded an abundance of plums, cherries, and pears. She boiled a pot of water for tea and poured a cup of cold milk at each setting. After removing the biscuits and tarts from the oven, she placed a pot of cream on the table.

Outside, Father Landry spoke to Papa in low tones by the chicken yard.

"I don't want to startle the girls, François, but I do not sense the ships in the harbour are here on a friendly mission."

"Why do you say that, Father? We're not their enemy. We're neutral."

"I overheard some of them talking—poking fun at us for being Catholic. The soldiers removed all the sacred objects from the church and set up headquarters. Lieutenant Colonel John Winslow is living in my house. They don't seem friendly. I sense the soldiers are here to bring harm."

"I'm sure they simply want us to reconsider the oath, Father. After all, this is British territory now. What was it the oath said—the one our fathers took in 1713?"

Father Landry looked up at the sky as if the words were written there.

"We certify we are exempt from bearing arms and promise never to bear arms against the English crown."

"There. You see?" Papa placed a strong, worn hand on the priest's shoulder. "We mean no harm to the English. We are neutral."

"Yes, but remember, they wanted us to take another oath, one that promised we would be entirely faithful and obey His Majesty King George II as Lord of Acadia."

"But Father Landry, when our ancestors were previously under English rule, they were never required to swear such an oath."

Father Landry nodded.

"At any rate, they are keeping the sisters terribly busy feeding them. There are at least 300 troops. I have been informed that they will need a portion of our harvests, and it is the responsibility of the village to feed them."

"Try not to worry, Father. We will do as they wish."

The priest's face looked grim. Francois looked up at the window where he saw Belina smile and wave them inside.

"Let's go in, shall we? My daughter is excited to share her turnip and potato pie."

The family gathered around the table and, after they said their prayers, gave the sign of the cross. Belina proudly served her meal.

"Mmmm, Mademoiselle Belina. Delicious! You will make a good sister of the church one day."

Father Landry patted his belly.

"Papa, Father wants me to become a *nonne*. I told him I cannot."

"Very well, my Belina. You shall become the mother of a dozen wailing children, is that it? Do you have a beau?"

Papa winked at Mama and ruffled Belina's hair.

"No, Papa. You are my only beau." Belina kissed her papa on the cheek and refilled his mug with milk.

"I am a blessed man. Two beautiful women to claim as my own." Papa smiled at Mama.

Mama blushed. "I have an announcement to make, if it is acceptable to you, Monsieur Thibodeaux."

François grinned. "*Oui*. Children, Mama has something to tell you."

"Is it a surprise?" Jean-Baptiste loved surprises.

Mama nodded. *"Oui,* Jean-Baptiste. You have a big responsibility now."

Belina gasped. She knew what her mother would say, but held her tongue to give Mama the honor of announcing it.

"I have a new job?" Jean-Baptiste spoke with a mouthful of pie.

Papa nodded. *"Oui.* A very, very important one."

"Well, don't keep me in suspense!" Father Landry leaned in toward Madame Thibodeaux. "Tell me the news!"

Mama grinned. "Father Landry, you will need to prepare for a baptism on Christmas Day."

Jean-Baptiste looked confused. "That is my job? I will baptize someone?"

Mama laughed. *"Non.* But you will be the big brother at the ceremony."

"Big brother?" Jean-Baptiste sat silent a moment and his eyes grew bigger. *"Un bébé, Mama?"*

"Oui." Mama smiled. "You have an important job now as a big brother."

Belina squealed and clapped. *"Hourra! Un bébé!* I can hardly wait, Mama." She ran to her mother and wrapped her arms around her.

"We need to dance! Papa, play your violin, *s'il vous plaît?"*

"Oui!" Monsieur Thibodeaux drew the *violon* out of the wooden box and rosined his bow, as Belina and Jean-Baptiste cleared the table.

Belina guided Mama to her chair by the hearth.

"You stay seated, Mama. We will do the dishes tonight and put the animals to bed."

"I'm not sick, I'm with child." Mama laughed and let out a long sigh. "But I am quite tired from making candles in the sun today."

Monsieur Thibodeaux played a cheerful dance tune with one foot on the table bench. Belina hooked her arm with Jean-Baptiste and they twirled around the room. Father Landry clapped and laughed and tapped his toe. There was joy and happiness in Acadia that night. No one could predict how quickly the joy that rang through the village would soon disappear like autumn leaves on sleepy trees.

ଔ

Days passed and life for Belina went on as usual. Work on the colonial farm was endless. Besides the daily milking of Nicole, gathering eggs, and caring for the other animals, there were the garden and fields to harvest. After the barley and rye were harvested, she helped her mother gather and dry herbs, while her father and brother harvested salt-marsh hay to feed the animals over the winter months. While other colonists butchered their animals for the winter because they had no way to feed them, Acadians were able to grow large herds. There was always plenty of meat, cheese, and milk to keep them strong and healthy.

There was also the need to help neighbors gather their crops, and everyone pitched in as needed. Wheat, oats, peas, corn, flax, and hemp were harvested by hand with scythes in the fields. In Mama's garden there were beets, carrots, parsnips, onions, chives, shallots, herbs, salad greens, cabbages, and turnips growing in profusion. No one at that time on earth had perfected such prosperous farming techniques.

Belina noticed Mama's growing discomfort and how taxing the outdoor work became as the baby grew. She gladly worked harder to help with some of her mother's chores. There was plenty to be done even while sitting down, and her mother spun wool and made clothes for the new baby.

On Sundays they attended church with all their friends at Monsieur Richard's house. The families were happy to be together as always on Sundays, but looked forward to the day when they could worship again in their own little church in Grand-Pré. Father Landry baptized Monsieur and Madame LeBlanc's twin girls and the Mi'kmaq Native, Monsieur White Owl, who chose to become a Catholic because of the kindness shown him by Father Landry, when a moose broke his foot.

They spent all day Sunday at Monsieur Richard's house, and Belina played with her best friend, Veronique. They owned no toys, but made necklaces and bracelets from dried wildflowers and straw, and dolls by fashioning an apple to a corncob. They made a fluffy bed with their bonnets by filling them with the downy soft fruits of cattails and wove little baskets for beds from the dry leaves.

Too soon it was time to go home and do chores. Even on Sunday, Nicole needed to be milked and animals had to be brought in from the pasture and put to bed.

"*Au revoir,* Veronique. See you next Sunday! Or maybe sooner if we can talk our Mamas into tea."

"Mademoiselle Belina, would you please take care of my daughter, Collette, until I return from my trip to France?"

Veronique pretended to need a babysitter for her new doll.

"*Oui,* Madamoiselle, and you my son Fabien, until I return from the lower colonies?" The girls giggled, embraced, and kissed one another on the cheek. They exchanged baskets and walked home with their families.

Belina could hear Nicole crying to be milked before she got home. The uncomfortable cow stood by the farmyard gate, waiting impatiently for her mistress.

"I'm coming, Nicole, *chérie.* Be patient while I put my new *enfant* to bed."

After putting her doll on her pillow, Belina helped Mama settle into her chair, while Jean-Baptiste restarted the fire in the hearth. Papa went out to the barn to help with the cattle and his horse, while Belina milked Nicole.

"*Ma chérie,* you have plenty of milk tonight. What a good, *gentille* cow you are."

Belina rested her head against Nicole's side and closed her eyes, listening to the rhythm of the milk hitting the wooden pail.

Finally, after several hours of chores, Belina was able to crawl into her bed in the loft. She could hear Mama and Papa whispering below.

Mama yawned.

"My dear husband, what were you and the men talking about today?"

"Do not worry my darling wife. There are only rumors. But Monsieur Gaudet said that…"

Belina didn't hear anything more. She was too tired and, before she knew it, Nicole was at the gate again, crying to be milked.

September 2, 1755

Belina's mama put her finishing touches on the new lamb's wool *couverture* for the new baby. Belina admired the delicate flowers her mother had embroidered along the edge.

"Oh, Mama, the blanket is beautiful. The baby will love it."

There was a loud knock at the door, and an English soldier stepped inside without giving Belina a chance to open the door.

"I am to deliver a message from Lieutenant Colonel John Winslow to all men and lads over the age of ten."

Belina scowled. How rude of this soldier to enter her house without being invited.

Mama's lip quivered as she stood tall by her chair.

"My husband is down by the dikes, helping Monsieur Boudreau."

The soldier turned and left without a good-bye.

Mama stared at the door.

"Belina, run to your papa and tell him what just happened. Then, go to Veronique's house and tell her mama to pass the word, too. After that, run as fast as you can and bring Father Landry to me."

"Why, Mama? What's wrong?"

Belina's mother walked to the window and rested a protective hand on top of her stomach.

"I don't know, Belina. But it can't be good news when a soldier enters my home uninvited."

Belina grabbed a shawl and ran to find her father. She passed by Jean-Baptiste, who carried a young lamb.

"Where are you going, Belina?" Jean-Baptiste yelled.

"Jean-Baptiste, go to Mama and stay there until Papa comes home."

Jean-Baptiste ran in the house with the lamb in his arms. Belina never spoke to him in that tone unless it was serious.

The fall day was blustery and cold; Belina hugged the shawl closer. She could taste sea salt on her lips even this far from shore. Her wooden shoes thumped one after the other, and Belina felt she couldn't run fast enough. She wanted to reach her papa before the soldier. She went by way of the trees and ignored the tempting fall crocuses peeking up with bright purple faces from underneath the cover of red and orange maple leaves. Normally she would have stopped to pick a bouquet for her mother. But not today.

"Papa!" She hollered at her father in the distance.

He immediately stopped digging and turned toward the sound of her voice. He ran toward her shouting, "Is it Mama?"

"No, Papa, not Mama, but a soldier with a message for you and Jean-Baptiste."

Papa ran. He shouted toward his friend, "Monsieur Boudreau, I must go home! Soldiers."

Monsieur Boudreau dropped his shovel and ran.

"Papa, I must go to Veronique's mother and to fetch Father Landry."

Belina ran beside her father as he ran toward home.

"Go, Belina, run fast. I'll go to Mama and Jean-Baptiste."

Belina kicked off her wooden shoes and, with one in each hand, ran away from her papa toward Veronique's house. She skipped over creeks and cut through fields that once held the harvests of barley and wheat. She wound her way past the dikes her father had helped to build and along the river's edge until she reached her best friend's house.

"Veronique! Veronique!"

Belina banged on the door. No one seemed to be around.

"Veronique!"

Belina ran to the back of the house and found Veronique and her mother, stirring clothes in a cauldron over a fire. It was washing day.

"Veronique! Madame Richard! I have a message from my mother."

"What is it child? Is it her time?"

Madame Richard wiped her hands on her apron and guided Belina toward the house.

"*Non.* My mother told me to tell you that soldiers are going house to house with a message. She wants you to pass the word and to pray."

"*Oui.* Come in and warm yourself before you head home."

The kind woman continued to guide Belina to the house.

Belina pulled away.

"*Non.* I must fetch Father Landry as my mother wishes."

"*Oui.* Tell your mother we are praying. I will send Veronique one direction, and I will go the other. Veronique, get your shawl."

Veronique pointed to the cauldron of boiling water.

"But Mama, the clothes…"

"Tell your brother to put the fire out. Go!"

Belina ran toward the church to find Father Landry. When she arrived she was overwhelmed at the sight of soldiers in red coats, walking inside and outside the picket fence they had erected the first week of their arrival. She looked for Father Landry and could find him nowhere.

"*Père Landry? Est-ce-que vous làvez vu?*" she asked a soldier who didn't look much older than herself.

He glared and spoke with venom in his voice.

"*Aucun français. Parler en anglais.* No French. Speak English."

Belina was afraid. She had never been spoken to in this tone. But she understood a little English. She searched her mind for the words.

"Fa..Fa-thuh Joseph?"

The soldier pointed toward the woods, and Belina ran to the clearing by the creek where she knew he liked to pray. As she ran, two white-tailed deer peeked out from among the birch trees.

"Père Landry! Père Landry!"

Belina's foot landed on a sharp rock, leaving a tiny trail of dark red blood drops atop the bright orange leaves covering the forest floor. She ran with her head down and collided with a solid object covered in an itchy wool robe.

"M'enfant, I am here. What is wrong?"

Father Landry put his hands on Belina's shoulders and leaned down to look into her eyes.

Belina panted and worked to catch her breath.

"A soldier came to our house today. He did not knock. Mama needs you."

Father Landry nodded. "We will go to her through the woods."

Father Landry ran behind Belina, who was a strong runner. Her back and legs remained strong after running for miles. The middle-aged priest had difficulty keeping pace with her long strides.

They arrived at the back of the house in time to see soldiers standing at the front door. Belina pulled Father Landry toward the oven lean-to and peeked around the corner. Her papa stood in the yard as a soldier read from a long parchment:

"To the inhabitants of the district of Grand Pré, Minas, River Canard and places adjacent:

"...both old and young men, as well as the lads of ten years of age, [are] to attend the church at Grand-Pré, on Friday, the 5th instant, at three in the afternoon, that we may impart to them what we are ordered to communicate to them, declaring that no excuse will be admitted on any pretense whatsoever, on pain of forfeiting goods and chattle, in default of real estate."

"What does that paper mean, Father Landry?"

Belina couldn't understand all the English words.

Father Landry put his finger to his lips. "Shh, my Belina. We will wait until they leave, and I will tell you."

They watched the soldiers march away and, when the last redcoat rounded the tree-lined bend, Belina and the priest scurried into the house.

"Mama! Papa! Father Landry is here."

They ducked inside and Belina shut the door.

"What was said, my husband?"

The dread on her mother's face made Belina feel afraid. Her body trembled.

Papa sat at the table and pulled Jean-Baptiste near him.

"My English is not that good. Father Landry, did you hear what they said?"

Father Landry nodded. Belina noticed his eyes did not dance as usual.

"Oui."

"Did they say we must go to the church tomorrow—all men and lads—at three o'clock?"

"Oui."

Suzette walked to her husband and put her arm around him.

"And if they do not?"

Father Landry sighed and looked down at the floor.

"They will seize your home and lands and animals."

No one spoke. Belina couldn't move. Her feet were cold and bleeding, but she still held her wooden shoes in her hands. Finally Papa spoke.

"Mama, what's for supper? Let's have a feast and dance. Belina, do you still have a run in you?"

"Oui, Papa."

"Run to Veronique's family and invite them to dinner. Afterwards we will dance!"

That night, the Thibodeaux and Richard families ate together and afterward Papa played the violin while Monsieur Richard played the mouth harp. Mama sat in her chair by the fire and pretended to smile, but Belina could see the concern in her mother's face. She watched Mama's hands as they rested on her round belly and moved the rosary bead by bead through her prayerful fingers.

"Do not worry, Madame Thibodeaux. God is with us."

Father Landry patted Mama on the shoulder, but she didn't stop praying.

September 5, 1755

Even though Nicole bellowed to be milked as usual the next morning, Belina could feel the day would be different. She did her chores and helped Mama in the kitchen. She set the table for lunch and helped Jean-Baptiste gather the sheep, pretending that three o'clock would never come.

But the dreadful time did arrive, and Papa kissed Mama good-bye, and Jean-Baptiste hugged Belina and kissed his mama.

"Don't worry, Mama." Jean-Baptiste stood tall and brave.

"Belina promised to make me a big supper of chicken fricot, and I will eat it all."

"*Oui*, my son. We will eat to the gills. Your new sibling is hungry."

Mama patted her tummy.

Belina hugged her Papa. "Tonight I'm going to make your favorite desert: *Poutines à trou.*"

Papa's mouth watered, imagining the sweet fruit pastry. "*Oui.* Make me three."

He held up three fingers.

Mama handed them a basket of fresh bread and cheese and a large jug of milk.

"Take this with you in case your meeting goes long."

Papa smiled and kissed his beautiful wife on the cheek. Belina watched them walk away until they grew too small to see.

September 10, 1755

Belina's tears fell onto Nicole's brindle coat as she leaned her head against the patient cow's soft belly and milked her. It had been five days since Papa and Jean-Baptiste had gone to the church. Monsieur Grangier came to the house after the soldiers let 20 prisoners free to tell the women of their plight. He told Mama and Belina that the English had taken them prisoner and it was up to the women of Grand-Pré to feed them and the soldiers. If Monsieur Grangier didn't return, they would kill one of the prisoners.

Belina wiped her eyes remembering Monsieur Grangier's words.

"When we arrived and were seated, they read an edict. There were more than 400 of us."

The dejected man fought his tears.

Mama reached over and patted his hand.

"What did this edict say?"

"I cannot say for sure. Only what Father Landry told me. They read it in English."

Monsieur Grangier wiped his eyes with his hands.

Belina felt impatient.

"What did Father Landry say it said?"

Reading the Order of expulsion to the Acadians in the parish Church at Grand-Pré, in 1755. Painting by Charles William Jefferys (1869-1951) 1923

"He said the King demanded we leave our homes with only what we can carry. Everything else–our homes, our land, our animals– it all belongs to the King of England."[3]

"But why?"

Belina felt angry. What right did a king have to take her Papa and brother from her?

105

"They think we are a threat to them."

Monsieur Grangier shook his head.

"It makes no sense. We have never taken up arms. We have always been neutral."

"Where will we go?" Mama cried, and tears fell upon the rosary she held in her hands.

"Wherever their ships are commanded to take us," Monsieur Grangier whispered, putting his head in his hands. He could do nothing but weep.

For days Mama wouldn't stop crying, but Belina took care to dry her own tears before she came into the house. She did her crying when she was out of doors, which was most of the time, now that there was no help with the animals. Mama's arms were strong and she made bread and worked tirelessly to provide hearty meals for the men of Grand-Pré who were now prisoners in their beloved church. Every day Belina filled a cart of milk and food which a prisoner would take to the church where even Father Landry was held captive.

On the eighth day there was a knock on the door. Monsieur DuPuis stood shivering in the brisk morning wind.

"Come in, Monsieur DuPuis. Sit at my table."

Mama immediately poured a mug of milk, tore off a generous piece of bread and slathered it with butter and honey.

"Merci." Monsieur DuPuis ate as if he hadn't eaten in days.

"Do they not feed you the food we send?" Mama sounded angry.

106

"I am not a prisoner. I've been hiding in the woods. I came here to tell you bad news."

Mama gasped and her hands flew to her stomach.

"My baby cannot take more bad news, Monsieur DuPuis."

"*Pardonnez-moi,* Madame. I am only the messenger. I did not bring this upon us."

Mama turned away and put her fist to her lips.

Belina handed him a bowl of stew.

"What is wrong, Monsieur DuPuis. Tell me."

"They are dividing the younger men, twenty-four to a ship, to detain them there. The soldiers are afraid they will revolt if they do not."

"*Non!*"

Mama ran out the door and collapsed in the yard.

"Mama, come back." Belina followed after her and found her mama beating the ground.

"*Non.* Not Jean-Baptiste. *Non, non, non.*"

Mama couldn't be consoled, and Belina held her as she wept, rocking back and forth on the ground.

As word spread, women and girls of Grand-Pré gathered along the road from the trail to the bay where the ships were docked. Mama found the arms of Madame Richard who held on to her and let her cry. Belina found Veronique, and they cried together for their fathers and brothers.

Then Belina kicked off her wooden shoes and ran to the church. She wouldn't let the soldiers take her brother. She couldn't.

"Belina! Where are you going?" Veronique shouted behind her, but Belina continued to run. At the church house gate, soldiers pushed her and she fell to the ground. Hundreds of soldiers stood between her and the door of the church as they lined up on each side of the young Acadian men.

"Ne pas sans nos pères! Not without our fathers!" Belina heard Pierre cry out. Her heart burst with pride at his bravery. She could see his hand upon Jean-Baptiste's shoulder, who did his best to choke back sobs.

Lt. Col. John Winslow shouted, "I do not understand French. I only understand what the king has ordered. Orders are orders and must be obeyed. Soldiers! Fix your bayonets!"

Belina watched as the English soldiers pointed their bayonets at the young Acadian men, who had no choice but to march the mile-and-a-half from the church to the ships. Pierre started singing and other young men joined, but many cried and others prayed. Women and children stood on each side of their beloved sons and husbands and brothers with their arms outstretched, falling upon their knees and weeping.

Every day Belina filled her cart with cheese and milk and her mother's freshly baked bread. For five long weeks the little stove and outdoor oven cooked and baked from sunrise to sunset. Belina fished for lobsters, butchered and plucked chickens, cared for the animals, and milked Nicole, who kindly gave her milk twice a day. She prayed endlessly for her brother and wondered if he could see the sun inside the belly of the great ship with which she had once been fascinated.

Now the houses on the water were monsters that had swallowed up two people she dearly loved: Jean-Baptiste and her friend, Pierre. Soon, the behemoth would swallow up Papa, Mama, and Belina too. Her heart filled with fear, she cried out every night to God and promised to become a *nonne,* if only God would keep them safe.

October 8, 1755

"Embark!"

Belina helped her mother as they finished loading their cart in the snow. It was difficult to know what to choose, but Mama decided wisely, taking only clothing and food. Her precious dishes, her furniture – none of their precious treasures could go with them.

As far as Belina could see, the families of the men imprisoned on the ships and at the church walked toward the bay. The elderly rode in carts pushed by strong young women, who also carried those who had no carts and could not walk.

Belina's cart started to tip over, and three soldiers pushed her mother out of the way to steady it.

"Don't touch my mother! She is with child."

The soldiers couldn't understand Belina's French. Instead they pushed a strong boy to the cart and ordered him to push it. In the scuffle, Belina got separated from her mother and friends.

Papa's violin lay on the snowy ground, and Belina picked up the precious instrument and hugged it to herself. When she looked for her Mama, she couldn't find her.

"Mama!" she shouted as loud as she could, but many young women and children cried for their mothers. Soldiers separated them and pushed them into separate lines to board separate ships. Belina sat on the ground and cried. And then she stood and slowly stepped backwards toward a stand of trees. As she looked behind herself, she spotted her Papa and Father Landry.

Papa put his fingers to his lips. She tucked the violin inside her shawl and crept backwards to her father, dodging the wheels of carts and wagons. At her papa's side, he whispered into her ear.

"Run, Belina, to those trees there. Run and hide and don't come out until we are gone."

"Non! Papa, I cannot leave you."

"Belina, the journey on the ship is long. I will find Mama and Jean-Baptiste, and we will come back for you. Now go, while you can. Run!"

Belina continued to back up and, while soldiers were distracted by Father Pierre who pretended to turn his ankle, Belina kicked off her wooden shoes and ran with tears flowing down her face more forceful than the river. She ran until she was far from the bay and her legs would no longer move.

On the mossy floor of the forest sprinkled with fresh snow, she curled into a ball and shook with fear. She curled her frozen feet beneath herself and wept. She felt confused. How had this happened to her happy home? Would she ever see her parents and brother again? She hugged the *violon* and rocked. And then it struck her.

110

Nicole! Nicole needed milking. The dear cow would wonder where she was.

Belina stood on shaky legs and ran back through the trees to the barn, but when she arrived she found the house and barns in flames. She clapped her hand over her mouth to stifle her screams. Her beloved chickens, Mama's quaint house with all of Papa's beautiful furniture—all of their things were gone. Nothing was left in Grand-Pré but a cloud of smoke.

Belina writhed in agony on the ground and held the violin close. The instrument was all she had of her family. She feared it was all she would have ever again.

Cʒ

That night, tucked in beneath a rosehip bush, Belina dreamed Nicole woke her as usual for milking and she awoke and milked her and did her chores. But no matter how much she milked her, the friendly cow wouldn't stop crying. Finally, Belina woke. The moon was high above her, but the sun was beginning to rise. The sounds of Nicole crying filled her ears. She shivered violently and realized she was hungry.

As she made her way back to the stream at the rear of her house, she heard sticks snapping behind her. She froze. Soldiers were still about Grand-Pré . What would the Redcoats do if they found her in the woods?

She turned to see who lurked behind her and got ready to run.

"Moo!"

"Nicole! Oh my dear sweet milk cow, you are okay!"

"Moo!"

"Shhh, *chérie Nicole calme.*" Belina stroked the traumatized cow's side. "You must be miserable. Come, let me milk you."

Nicole milked the cow, letting her precious milk spill to the ground. Belina filled the mug tied to a rope around her neck and drank deep. Nicole mooed in appreciation and, when the milking was done, Belina got on her knees and said her prayers. When she finished, she led Nicole through the woods.

"Come, Nicole. We must find our way. I don't know where we are going, but when we get there, we will know."

A large hand clasped across her mouth and strong arms fought to keep her from screaming and running away. She hadn't seen the dark figure watching her from behind a raspberry bush.

"Shhh, my dear. Quiet."

Belina's body raged with adrenaline. As the violin fell to the snowy ground, she clawed at the hand and kicked her feet. The other arm of the stranger reached around her and dangled wooden shoes in front of her face.

Her shoes? Who had found her shoes?

She wiggled her head up to see her attacker.

Father Landry!

When he saw the recognition in her eyes, he let go.

"Father Landry!" Belina hugged him, and he held her

trembling body up so she could stand.

"Oh Father Landry, the soldiers burned my house, and my chickens and sheep are all gone."

"I know, *ma chérie.*" He held the girl and let her cry.

"Where did the ships take my family?"

Father Landry shook his head.

"I heard the ships went different places. I escaped during the night before they embarked."

Belina's eyes filled with more tears. How many tears did one little girl store inside? Surely she had spent them all.

"But where did they go?"

"To the British Colonies, I think." Father Landry stroked Nicole's back.

Belina looked into the priest's sad eyes. "Will I ever see them again?"

Father Landry couldn't answer. He only shook his head.

Belina sobbed. "Where will we go now, Father?"

"I don't know, dear Belina. But we will go with God."

"Can we take Nicole?"

"*Oui.* Nicole's milk will give us sustenance, and we can trade her milk for food and other things we need."

1767–New Orleans, Louisiana

Every morning Belina met the ships at port in New Orleans, looking into every face that disembarked until the sun disappeared behind the gulf's horizon. She silently prayed blessings on White Owl and Father Landry, who had protected her on their frightening journey to a small French colony in Louisiana in 1758. She held her rosary and prayed in between selling vegetables and flowers to passersby.

On a humid, dreary evening, as she packed her baskets and turned to walk away, she noticed two frail men stumbling toward the setting sun. Something in the shape of their shadows reminded her of a happy time in Acadia. Her heart jumped.

"Papa?" Belina whispered the word that had rested so long in her throat. "Papa? Is that you?"

She ran across the pier and leapt over a wagon of bananas sitting on the dock.

"Papa! Jean-Baptiste!"

The two hungry figures turned slowly and dropped the burdens they carried. Belina leapt into her father's arms.

"Ma chérie, Belina, thank God I've found you."

Papa embraced the sobbing girl who didn't want to let go. Were it not that Jean-Baptiste stood beside them crying her name, she wouldn't have.

She looked into Jean-Baptiste's eyes. He was no longer the little boy she'd once known but a man who wore sadness in his shoulders.

"Where's Mama?"

Belina searched their faces. They both shook their heads. Belina held on to her father and cried.

114

Papa stroked her hair.

"The voyages were too much for her. She died before the baby came, Belina, in her sleep. She did not suffer. She is in heaven now, waiting for us all."

Belina cried and made the sign of the cross. She had the hope of heaven and for now, that comfort needed to be enough.

Jean-Baptiste whispered, "Father Landry? Have you seen him? He wasn't on the ship."

"He lives with me in a little house on the Bayou. He mostly stays home and prays. The heat here is difficult for him. Come, Papa and Jean-Baptiste, let me take you home and make you some Rappie Pie. You look like you haven't eaten in years."

Belina picked up her father's satchel and started toward home.

"Belina, the *violon?* You still have it?"

"Oui, mon cher papa. I have learned to play a few melodies. You will be impressed."

Papa smiled and put his arm around Jean-Baptiste to help him walk.

"Then tonight you will play, and I will dance. It is good to be finally home."

August 28, 2005

"Beaux! Beaux! Where are you?"

Beaux Thibodeaux opened his eyes to darkness and the sound of water running. A flashlight beam illuminated the ceiling in the hall.

"I'm in here!"

A large, shirtless man with deep brown skin slogged through knee-deep water and found Beaux in his grandfather's bedroom. He picked the boy up like a sack of potatoes.

"I need my violin!"

The man handed the violin to Beaux, and they made their way outside to a waiting pirogue.

"Ga lee, Beaux Thibodeaux, your grandpapa and grandmama gone be glad to see you. You one lucky boy, you aks me."

"My old violin is sure glad to see you, Joe Landry."

Joe laughed and carried him to the pirogue and carefully placed Beaux and the violin inside. He rowed them both into the future, where the old violin would sometimes cry for places lost, and sometimes dance for happiness and dreams never known in New France.

Once again, the old violin found its way to safety. The fiddle had seen as many happy days as years of sadness. No longer Acadian, it now was Cajun and would sing the songs of an original and dynamic culture. It would forever sing the songs of old *Acadie.* **

**Note: the word "Cajun" is a pidgin variation of the word "Acadian", which has long been used by the Acadians who settled in Louisiana.

Endnotes:

[1] Did you know that there is no difference between a violin and a fiddle in the way they are made? They are the exact same instrument. The difference is in how they are played. Classical players usually refer to their instrument as a violin. Folk players call it a fiddle. But both players often use the term interchangeably.

[2] Acadians referred to lunch as dinner and the evening meal was supper. It is still this way in some parts of North America. When the author lived in Iowa, she showed up five hours late for a dinner when she should have arrived at noon. In the rural Iowa town in which she lived, lunch was a snack that farmer's wives took to the farmers in the fields at any time of the day. Refreshments at a meeting was also called lunch.

[3] The edict was a lie. The King of England did not order the removal. However, those he put in charge of that area of Canada did. The text of the edict reads as follows:

"Gentlemen, - I have received from His Excellency Governor Lawrance The King's Commission, which I have in my hand and by whose orders you are Convened together to Manifest to you His Majesty's Final Resolution to the French Inhabitants of this his Province of Nova Scotia who for almost half a Century have had more Indulgence Granted them than any of his Subjects in any part of his Dominions. What use you have made of them, you your Self Best Know.

The Part of Duty I am now upon is what thoh Necessary is Very Disagreable to my natural make & Temper as I Know it Must be Grevous to you who are of the Same Specia.

But it is not my Business to annimedvert, but to obey Such orders as I receive and therefore, without Hesistation Shall Deliver you His Majesty's orders and Instructions vizt.

That your Lands & Tenements, Cattle of all Kinds, and Live Stock of all Sortes, are Forfitted to the Crown with all other your Effects Saving your money and Household Goods and you your Selves to be removed from this his Province.

Thus it is Preremptorily His Majesty's orders That the whole French Inhabitants of these Districts, be removed, and I am Throh his Majesty's Goodness Directed to allow you Liberty to Carry of your money and Household Goods as Many as you Can, without

Discomemoading the Vessels you Go in. I Shall do Every thing in my Power that all Those Goods be Secured to you and that you are Not Molested in Carrying of them of and also that whole Familys Shall go in the Same Vessel. and make this remove, which I am Sensable must give you a great Deal of Trouble as Easey as His Majesty's Service will admit and hope that in what Ever part of the world you may Fall you may be Faithful Subjects, a Peasable & happy People.

I Must also Inform you That it is His Majesty's Pleasure that you remain in Security, under the Inspection & Direction of the Troops that I have the Honr. to Command."

At this point Winslow declared the Acadians the King's prisoners. He also ordered the following:

All officers and Soldiers and Sea Men Employed in his Majesty's Service as well as all his Subjects of what Denomination Soever, are herby Notifyed That all Cattle vizt Horsses, Horne Cattle, Sheep, goats, Hoggs, and Poultrey of Every Kinde. that was this Day Soposed to be Vested in the French Inhabitants of this Province are become Forfitted to his Majesty whose Property they now are and Every Person of what Denomination Soever is to take Care not to Hurt Kill or DistJoe anything of any Kinde nor to Rob Orchards or Gardens or to make waste of anything Dead or alive in these Districts without Special order.

LUCY MAUD MONTGOMERY
NOVEMBER 30, 1874 - APRIL 24, 1942

Fair Island of the sea,

We raise our song to thee,

The bright and blest;

Loyally now we stand

As brothers, hand in hand,

And sing God save the land

We love the best.

Upon our princely Isle

May kindest fortune smile

In coming years;

Peace and prosperity

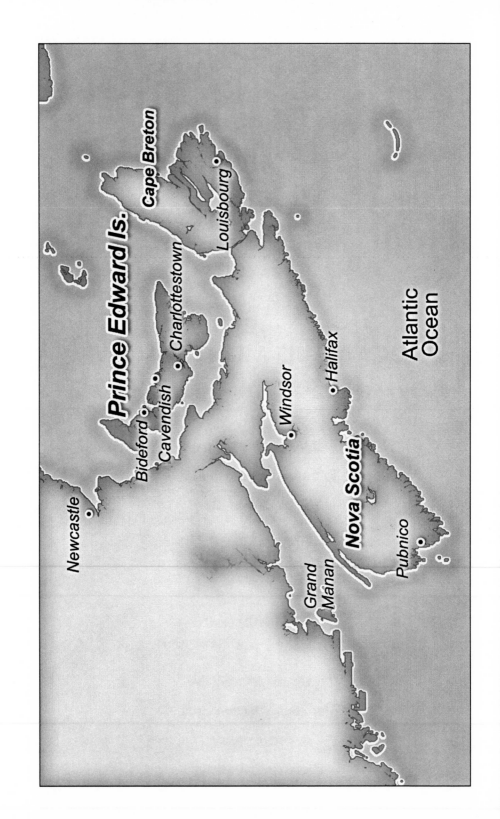

Fair Island of the sea,

We raise our song to thee,

The bright and blest;

Loyally now we stand

As brothers, hand in hand,

And sing God save the land

We love the best.

Upon our princely Isle

May kindest fortune smile

In coming years;

Peace and prosperity

In all her borders be,

From every evil free,

And weakling fears.

Prince Edward Isle, to thee

Our hearts shall faithful be

Where'er we dwell;

Forever may we stand

As brothers, hand in hand,

And sing God save the land

We love so well.

"The Island Hymn" by Lucy Maud Montgomery, 1908

Young Maud, Age 9

I squealed at the top of my lungs and lit out of the house like my hair was on fire when the carriage, pulled by four dusty horses, rattled up to our front door.

"Lucy Maud Montgomery, come back here and mind your manners. That is no way for a lady to act. Get inside so I can introduce you properly." Grandmother Macneill scowled and wagged her finger in my direction.

I slumped my shoulders, lowered my head, and clomped into the house. Grandmother Lucy Macneill didn't understand the nature of excitement. She didn't have the burden of being a little girl living alone with her discontented grandparents, having no one with whom to play. An old woman with no imagination couldn't possibly appreciate the overwhelming power of exuberance.

Grandmother greeted the carriage while I stood near the door jumping around like the baby rabbits in the cabbage patch. I clapped my hand over my mouth to keep from shouting my greetings to Wellington and David Nelson as they disembarked and politely introduced themselves to my grandmother.

Grandmother guided them to the front door where I stood with my hand firmly planted on my face.

"Gentlemen, this is my granddaughter, Maud. She stays here with her grandfather, Mr. Alexander Macneill and me because she is somewhat of an orphan like you two. Maud, these nice young gentlemen will be staying with us during the school year."

122

Grandmother frowned at me and raised her eyebrows. There was no pleasing her, was there?

The taller one grinned and removed his hat.

"Pleased to meet you. My name is Wellington, but you can call me Well."

The younger one tilted his freckled face and looked me square in the eye.

"Pleased to meet you. My name is David, but you can call me Dave. Why is your hand over your mouth?"

I removed my hand and sucked in air.

"Because I never know what's going to come popping out of it. My tongue seems to have a mind of its own, and Grandmother says I talk too much. I'm pleased to meet you too. My name is Maud. Without an *e* if you please."

I held out my hand and shook theirs.

Grandmother rolled her eyes.

"Come in and Maud-without-an-*e* can show you to your room."

She followed us into the house and we ran to the stairs.

"There will be no running in this house," Grandmother warned.

We slowed to a walk, but at the top of the stairs broke into a trot.

I showed the boys their room.

"You will stay here. My room is up there inside the gable. What's it like to be an orphan?"

The boys shrugged. Well scratched his head.

"No one's ever asked me before. I guess it's kind of sad, really."

Dave sat their tiny satchel of belongings on the bed.

"You should know what it feels like. You're an orphan."

"I'm not really an orphan. My father is still alive, but he works for the government in Western Canada. He has an extremely important job as a land developer. My mother died when I was two. That's when I moved to Cavendish on Prince Edward Island to live with my grandparents in this green-gabled house by the sea."

"It's not so near the sea, is it?"

Well looked out the window.

"It's not far, only a twenty-minute walk or so."

I reached into their satchel and unpacked the boys' belongings.

"Who are you named for?"

Well turned from the window and looked at the pictures on the wall. "What do you mean?"

I placed two well-worn shirts in the bureau.

"I was christened Lucy after my grandmother and Maud after one of Queen Victoria's daughters. I loathe the name Lucy and forbid anyone to call me such. Forevermore I shall be simply Maud, a much more romantic and proper name, wouldn't you agree?"

Dave looked at his brother who whispered in his ear, "Don't worry, Dave. She's a girl. Men aren't supposed to understand them."

Completely engrossed in my own conversation, I sat on the bed and continued, "I have so many things to tell you I scarcely

124

know where to begin. I suppose I should start with the death of my mother, Clara Woolner Macneill, whose funeral I am sad to say, I still remember."

"But you were only two. How can you remember?"

Well picked up a small rubber ball in a basket by the door and bounced it off the wall. Dave sat beside me on the bed.

"I have vivid memories of the coffin in the living room, the smell of musty tallow candles burning, and the coldness of my mother's skin when my father held me up to kiss her. I shudder thinking of it. Tender little girls with remarkable memories should not be asked to visit their mother's coffin."

Dave nodded.

"I don't remember when our parents died."

Well sat beside his brother and draped a protective arm around him.

"That's because you were just a baby. And I was only two. But I don't remember, either."

Grandmother's servant, Josephine, peeked into the room.

"Children, lunch will be ready in ten minutes. Wash up."

"Yes, ma'am."

The boys stood and went to the wash basin.

I followed and waited my turn.

"I feel it my duty to inform you that my grandmother has nothing to do with stuff and nonsense. My grandparents have already raised six children and don't allow noise in the house. Grandmother also says my imagination is too enthusiastic, but I think life would be dull and tedious without enthusiasm. What do you think?"

The boys shrugged and continued to wash their hands.

"Enthusiasm comes from the Greek, meaning 'God within.' If Grandmother would let me explain that to her, I'm sure she would change her mind and agree that my imagination is theologically correct. But a child doesn't discuss such revelations with her elders."

I took my turn at the wash basin.

"Grandmother doesn't have an imagination, and I think it must be dreadful. A life without imagination would be a greater calamity than I could possibly suffer. She thinks it's silly the way I name trees and flowers. After supper, I'll introduce you to some of them."

We made our way downstairs to the dining room. I could tell immediately that the boys had no idea how to use manners at the table. They watched me as I showed them how to place a napkin in their laps and hold their spoons properly. No one spoke because talking wasn't allowed at the table unless Grandmother was teaching manners.

"Don't slurp your soup, Well. You are not eating at a trough," Grandmother scolded.

"Yes, Ma'am."

After lunch, we helped Josephine clear the dishes, and I gave my new friends a tour outdoors.

"Do you see that little plum tree in the corner there by the fence?" I pointed to the far corner of the orchard.

Photo: Wikimedia / Public Domain / Lucy Maud as a child

"That's Little Syrup. And over on the other side of the lane are Spotty, Spider, and White Lady Birch. I'm quite sure the trees like their names. If I were a tree, I would want a name, wouldn't you? Come with me to the front yard to meet more of my friends."

We scampered to the front yard.

"Do you see how the maple and spruce tree have grown up together, entwined around each other? Those are 'The Lovers.' They must have loved one another deeply to embrace one another for eternity this way."

"Trees don't feel love," Well sighed, shaking his head.

I stomped my foot. "Then how do you explain their embrace?"

I marched to the front porch and pointed to my potted plant.

"This is Bonny. Isn't she the most splendid geranium you ever did see? Her petals are like puff sleeves on a beautiful pink dress. Do you see what I mean? I like things to have handles. I think it makes it a less lonely world."

Well sighed again, "Now I know why you placed your hand over your mouth when we came here."

I gave him my best Queen Victoria scowl.

"What do you mean by that?"

"You never stop talking."

"Before you came, I had no human children with whom to talk. Imagine how many words are stored up that have never had the opportunity to come out."

I threw up my hands for emphasis.

"It must get awfully lonely. The teachers at the orphanage are mean, but at least we have friends."

I liked knowing Well was sympathetic to my plight.

"I don't mind too terribly that I have no children friends. I have made friends of the trees, the creatures that wander in the woods, and my books and cats. I adore cats and kittens, don't you? They are such lovely, fluffy, understanding creatures. I once had a cat named Pussywillow who was my complete favourite. She was a beautiful gray like the sea in winter. She knew all my secrets. When she died from eating rat poison, I wanted to die too. Before then, I was a happy, unconscious little animal. From the time of her death, I began to have a soul. Want to know one of my secrets?"

The boys nodded.

I pulled back my long brown hair.

"Watch my ears. See? I can wiggle them! Not everyone can wiggle their ears as eloquently. Grandfather says it's a rare talent. I heartily agree. Can you wiggle yours?"

The boys tried to wiggle their ears, but their eyebrows only slid up and down like the paddle on Grandmother's butter churn.

I laughed and changed the subject.

"Don't you just love books? I learned to read when I was only three."

Dave sat on the stoop.

"I'm learning to read right now."

Well joined Dave on the stoop.

"Reading's okay. I'd rather fish. My grandparents have books in their library that I can read as often as I wish, except on Sundays. On Sundays I must sit completely still and am only allowed to read the Bible or *The Memoir of Anzonetta Peters.* I choose to read about Anzonetta. She is a perfect little girl who never makes mistakes. I long to be like her, but alas! I fail each day. I am often in trouble for tearing the lace on my dress, or coming to dinner with dirty hands. I'm not forgetful on purpose. The trouble with being forgetful is that one fails to remember one's forgetfulness. It's a quandary. Want to know another secret? I have two imaginary friends. Let's go inside and I'll introduce them to you. Step quietly. Grandmother doesn't like noise."

We made our way to the living room, and I sat in front of the oak cabinet with the glass doors.

"At night, the dancing lights from the fireplace are reflected in the gleaming windows. That's when I visit with Lucy Gray and Katie Maurice. Katie is a kindred spirit. We have much in common. We both love poetic, romantic things. She lives behind the right hand door."

"She lives in the cabinet?" Dave looked into the cabinet. "I don't see anything but dishes."

"That's because you haven't developed an imagination. There's also an unhappy, old woman named Lucy Gray who lives behind the left hand door. Even though she's grumpy, I remain her friend because she tells the most fascinating stories. Unfortunately, Lucy and Katie dislike one another and never speak. I try and try to get them to reconcile to no avail. It can get extremely tiring being in the middle, but alas, there's nothing to be done. Lucy will continue to be cross and difficult, and Katie will persevere and try not to let Lucy's nagging bother her."

"Do I hear children in the parlour?" Grandmother's voice rang near.

"Hide!"

We hid behind the long curtains, and I peeked between the panels and watched as Grandmother stuck her head in for a moment and then left.

"Whew, that was a close one," I breathed.

"What would happen if she found us?"

Dave's look of terror gave me sinister satisfaction. Perhaps boys could have an imagination after all.

"I shan't dare tell you," I whispered, "but trust me. You don't want to find out."

CC

The next morning I ran down a dusty trail sheltered by spruce trees. I had named this narrow road "Lover's Lane" and it was my favourite place to gather flowers. I was planning a picnic with Dave and Well. I had wanted them to join me, but they were being punished by Grandfather for wrestling.

"Dave's black eye won't look good on the first day of school," I spoke to the posies as I gathered them in my tiny hands. I was quite proud of my hands. Father said my hands were delicate and pretty like my mother's.

I picked a daisy and whispered, "At least Well's bloody nose won't be obvious."

"Are you talking to the flowers, Miss?" inquired Mr. Ogilby, one of my grandmother's servants, who was working in the garden nearby.

"Yes, Mr. Ogilby. Have you said hello to the vegetables for me?"

I believe even vegetables have souls.

"I have, Miss, and they asked me to wish you a good day."

Mr. Ogilby tipped his straw hat, and I waved at him as I skipped toward the house to make sandwiches for our picnic.

Inside, I could hear Grandmother moving about upstairs. Josephine was nowhere to be found. I placed my basket on the counter and went into the pantry for a jar of apple butter, where it sat out of my reach on a high shelf.

I sighed and spoke to the flowers in my basket, "If I ask grandmother to help me, she will scold me for my dirty shoes. And when I tell her I don't like to wear shoes, she will become cross."

I scanned the kitchen and my eyes rested on the old wooden bench against the wall. I pulled it into the pantry and climbed on top of the far end. If I stood on my tip-toes I could almost reach the coveted jar. As I stretched my hand toward it, the bench tottered. I lunged for something to grab and my hands fell on the cracker tin which went tumbling to the floor.

"Oh no. This is troubling."

I fell sideways, crashed into the pantry shelves, and Grandmother's canned peaches rained down on my head. The sound of breaking glass reverberated throughout all of Cavendish. I sat in a sea of peaches and glass, and when I looked up, Grandmother towered over me with her mouth open in the shape of a gaping arc. I immediately thought of the pictures I'd seen in one of Grandfather's books of a Triumphal Arch in Palestine. Thanks to my imagination, I was too fascinated by her look of horror to be concerned with Grandmother's wrath.

"Alexander! Come quickly!"

Grandmother stood with a hand on her forehead, looking up at

132

the ceiling. I looked up to see what was there. I saw nothing.

I heard Grandfather scuffle into the kitchen with his newspaper rustling. I groaned. Besides ruining all of Grandmother's peaches, I had interrupted his morning reading of the London Times.

He peeked into the pantry and pulled his pipe out of his mouth.

"What on earth are you doing there on the floor?"

"I wanted apple butter for a picnic," I declared loudly, because Grandfather was hard of hearing.

"Do you not know the difference between apple butter and peaches?"

Grandfather folded his paper and laid it on the table with his pipe as Grandmother pulled the bench out of the pantry.

"Give me your hands, slowly."

Grandfather reached for me. I was covered in peaches and glass, and as I stood, the slippery fruit slid down my back and into my dress.

"Careful now," Grandfather warned.

I picked my way out of the closet and Grandmother helped me remove my clothes. She wrapped me in a tea towel and placed a cold wet cloth on the bump on my head.

I couldn't read their faces. It seemed as if they were trying to hide a smile, but I thought the better of it. My imagination enjoyed playing tricks on me.

"I'm sorry."

Grandmother picked the peaches and glass out of my hair.

133

"It's done and there's nothing to do now but clean it up. Go on, change into a clean dress."

"Can I still go on a picnic with Well and Dave?"

"Please do, and stay out until supper time."

Grandfather plopped the pipe into his mouth, tucked his newspaper under his arm, and left the kitchen.

I couldn't believe my ears. I looked at Grandmother.

She rolled her eyes and waved me to the stairs.

"Go on, get dressed while I get your basket ready. But for penance you will help me with all the canning for the rest of the week."

"*All* the canning?"

I saw my summer fade into jar after jar of green beans, carrots, cherries, and whatever else grandmother decided to store for the winter.

"But it's the last week before school, and I have plans with Well and Dave."

Grandmother's glare sent me running up the stairs to change.

"What happened to you?" Well asked from the punishment chair in the hall.

Dave giggled from his assigned stool two doors down.

I shot them a pirate-glare as fierce as a buccaneer in Stevenson's *Treasure Island*.

"Shhhh. If you speak to me they will punish you longer."

I dashed to my room and slipped into my other dress. I didn't bother changing my peach-soaked stockings. They would get dirty anyway.

134

When we finally made it out of doors, we ran out of sight of my grandparents' house to the orchard. We spread a blanket on the mossy ground and feasted on clotted cream, scones, and apple butter sandwiches. We picked plums from the trees and ate until our tummies nearly burst.

"I'm tired now," Dave yawned, sprawling out on the blanket.

"Well, you can't go to sleep. The orchard and woods are haunted."

I folded our napkins carefully and placed them inside the basket beside my wilting flowers.

"I saw a ghost once," Well mumbled, while chewing on a piece of wheat grass, "in the orphanage attic."

"What were you doing in the attic?"

Dave's eyes were as big as the plums he'd eaten.

"Hiding from Mrs. Abernathy."

Dave nodded. "She's mean."

"What did the ghost look like?"

I stopped folding the napkins and sat on my knees looking at him.

"Well, I didn't actually see it myself. My friend Huntington did."

Well laid on his back and locked his hands behind his head.

"But from what he told me, it looked kind of like those clouds up there."

I looked at the sky and nodded.

"Then it was a ghost for sure. They are White Things. We have those here, you know. We also have fire animals, but they only come out at night and can't leave the woods. But the White Things can wander anywhere at all times of the day."

"Let's build a house and play castles."

Dave jumped up and gathered old wooden posts, sticks, and evergreen boughs.

"Okay, but I'm Queen Victoria and Well, you're Prince Albert."

I would not share the ruling of my kingdom, and besides, nothing was more fun to play than tragic fairy-tales.

"But he dies," Well said.

"Yes, you will die and I will mourn."

Boys never understood the important theatrics of dreadful misfortune.

"And Dave, you will be my son, the Prince of Wales."

"Okay," Dave shrugged and then continued to collect building materials.

We constructed our playhouse and spent hours playing out swashbuckling dramas similar to what I'd read in Sir Walter Scott's *Ivanhoe*. As Prince Albert lay dying from typhoid fever, something white caught my eye.

"Is that what I think it is?" I gasped, pointing to a grove of trees where I'd seen something move.

My ailing Prince sat up from his deathbed and looked toward the woods.

136

"What?"

"There!"

I gripped Dave's arm.

"I see it." Dave's face turned a little green.

"White Things," Well whispered. We sat staring at the place where'd we'd seen it move across the floor of the Haunted Woods.

"Where'd it go?"

Dave craned his neck to see if he could catch sight of it.

"Maybe it's the widow Anderson. She wanders in the woods all the time, you know." I tried to reassure myself as much as the boys.

"No! There it is again!" Well's voice shook with fear.

At the same time he spoke we saw a white shape move in the Haunted Woods. Without wasting a minute we ran screaming toward home. We were so convinced that something awful in the woods was after us that Mr. Ogilby grabbed a shovel and his wife grabbed a pitch fork and ran to find it. Grandmother took us inside and sat us down at the kitchen table. We were trembling like newborn calves.

Grandfather laughed watching us shiver.

"So you met a real ghost out there in the Haunted Woods did you? Tell me all about it."

We all spoke at once and grandfather sat across from us with his eyes twinkling. How could he be amused by such a horrifying event?

Josephine served us cold glasses of milk and generous slices of potato spice cake. Afterwards, Grandmother ordered us up to our rooms for naps.

"You're overwrought. Go upstairs and rest until supper."

I couldn't bear to be in my room alone and sneaked into the boys' room as soon as I heard Grandfather snoring through the vent in the floor.

I took the boys' hands in mine and looked into their eyes the same as I imagined Juliet looked at her beloved Romeo in Shakespeare's romantic play, except for the being in love part. Mostly I used the earnest part.

"We must always remember this day for it's the day we saw the ghost of the Haunted Woods. I know I shan't ever forget it as I have a vivid memory, but you haven't my gift for remembrance and must work at it. You must promise me you will not forget."

The boys nodded and we huddled against the wall underneath the window holding hands.

"What if it comes into our room tonight?" Dave whimpered.

"I have never heard of a White Thing coming into a house. I'm not sure it likes houses."

I wasn't convinced that was true, but Dave was younger than me, and needed reassurance.

At supper that evening, as Mrs. Ogilby served the cod fish soup, Grandmother asked, "Did you bring in the wash, Mrs. Ogilby? It looks like it might rain."

"Yes, Mum."

"Good. I'm glad I remembered to bring in the big white table cloth I had set out in the sun to dry. I almost forgot about it. The wind had blown it all the way into the Haunted Woods."

慓

Grandmother had mercy on me after the second day of canning. She said my constant prattling gave her the nerves and I was more work than help. She sent me with Well and Dave to fish on the Lake of Shining Waters.

"You can bait a hook? I've never seen a girl bait a hook before." Well seemed intrigued regarding my acquaintance with worms.

"Of course I can. I'm a girl, not an idiot."

I plopped my line into the lake and waited for a willing fish. The air was stifling and the water didn't move. "I think it's too hot for the fish to bite."

"We could fish later and go for a swim instead." Well pulled in his line.

"Okay!" Dave removed the worm from his fishing hook and flung it into the water.

I wiped the perspiration from my neck.

"I can't disagree. Let's go."

We ran to the beach and played along the ocean waves. I couldn't swim and stayed close to the shore and let the waves soak and cool me. The Canadian sea water was far too cold for swimming anyway. But the boys knew how to swim and ventured further out.

"I'm hungry," Dave grumbled, rubbing his tummy as he came in from a swim.

"We're all out of sandwiches," I replied, pointing to the empty basket that once held our lunch. "Let's find some dulse."

We ran along the shore, gathering sea shells and stopping to watch water fowl, star fish and crabs. We found a bountiful crop of dulse along the rocks farther down shore. Its salty leaves were delicious, and when we went home our tummies barely had room for supper.

"Maud, are you sure you want to go to school?" Grandfather Macneill, who rarely spoke, questioned me before lighting his pipe. "Most girls don't go to school after learning to read, and you've practically read my entire library."

"I think it's important for a girl to get an education, Grandfather. I want to be a writer and a writer needs to know lots of things."

"Let her go to school," Grandmother answered as she lit the lamps. "At least if she's at school we know where she is, and she's not chattering us into the grave."

I loved learning, but school wasn't as much fun as I thought it might be. Grandmother sewed all my clothes and the other girls made fun of me and called them "baby aprons."

"I'd give anything for a pretty dress," I confided to Well on the way home from school.

"I'd give anything to be as smart as you. You know more than anybody in the whole school. You're awfully smart, Maud."

I shrugged.

"I'm not smart on purpose. Everything I know I learned from reading. It doesn't take a genius to read a book."

"Mr. Peters is a hard teacher," frowned Dave. "He smacked my hands because I couldn't get my sums right, but I tried as hard as I could."

"Teachers shouldn't smack little boys' hands, Dave. I'll help you with your sums, okay?"

I placed a motherly arm around Dave and looked at the marks on the back of his hands.

"I'll fix your hands right up with one of Josephine's salves when we get home."

Well shuddered.

"I nearly got into trouble when Mr. Peters thought I was using slang. But it was Albert, not me, and Albert got the stick."

"That's a silly rule. Sometimes I think teachers make up rules to feel powerful, don't you? If I were a teacher I wouldn't make impractical rules. I would simply help children learn to read and let them use their imaginations."

The next day at school, Mr. Peters asked about the War of 1812.

"What was the result of the Americans' planned attack on Canadians at Beaver Dam?"

I raised my hand. Mr. Peters pointed to me. I stood.

"Thanks to the bravery of Laura Secord, we won."

"Explain, Miss Montgomery," Mr. Peters returned. He always formally addressed his students.

"She overheard the plan of attack while quartering American soldiers. She escaped from the house by the skin of her teeth and ran barefoot all the way from Queenston to Fitz Gibbon's headquarters at the Decew house."

Mr. Peters glared at me and demanded, "What did you say?"

"Laura Secord…"

"No, before that. You used slang, and what are the rules regarding slang?"

"I didn't use slang, sir. I never use slang."

"You did. You said 'by the skin of her teeth.' That is slang." Mr. Peters retorted while retrieving his cane from the wall.

"No sir, I did not. 'Skin of my teeth' is in the Holy Scriptures."

"You dare to question your teacher and assume you know more than I?"

"I do, sir, because you are wrong. Job 19:20." I glowered.

Mr. Peters' eyebrows climbed up his forehead like two enormous feathers and nearly reached his hair line.

"Come here, young lady."

I lifted my chin and walked forward to the teacher's desk. He could punish me, but he was still wrong. And I would not cry.

"Put your hands on my desk."

142

I looked him straight in the eye and placed my hands on the worn wooden desk. While all my peers watched, he whipped me. Even with my vivid memory, I can't precisely remember how many blows I took, but I do remember I was unable to keep my promise not to cry. By the ninth or tenth blow, I could stand the pain no more.

Well and Dave helped me home after school. Every step I took sent searing pain like fire through my legs and back.

"Please don't tell my grandparents," I whimpered.

"But you must tell them. You were right and he was wrong."

Well's tears fell off his eyelashes and slid down his nose.

I shook my head.

"Grandmother will say I earned the whipping for speaking my mind. She is always telling me to keep my thoughts to myself."

"I'll do your chores tonight, Maud."

Dave's voice was so sympathetic I couldn't help but weep. I had two friends who were kindred spirits. Though my body throbbed with pain, my heart leapt for joy.

Maud Grows Up

My father married Mary Ann MacRae, and after my little sister, Kate, was born, he sent for me. That meant saying good-bye to my friends, Well and Dave. But my imagination was eager to experience the West, and I looked forward to seeing my father again.

My other Grandfather, Senator Montgomery, rode with me on the train that took us to Saskatchewan. We disembarked in Regina and endured a terribly bumpy stage coach ride to the town of Prince Albert. Grandfather was eager to meet his new daughter-in-law and grandchild. But the new Mrs. Montgomery was not eager to meet me.

I had barely unpacked my trunk when Mrs. Montgomery handed me a long list of duties. "Here is a list of your chores. I expect them to be done each day in exactly this order."

"What about my studies?" I entreated, staring at the list.

"Studies will not make you a good wife. That is your first duty. Get going. I expect this list completed before your father comes home."

Mrs. Montgomery hugged her large stomach and sat on the couch. She was expecting another child.

My chores increased more each day. I felt more like a servant than a daughter, but I never disrespected my stepmother, nor let my father know. I missed my beloved Prince Edward Island with its beautiful seashore, brilliant green fields, and fiery red dunes.

I was finally allowed to go to school, but it was completely different from school in Cavendish. Prince Albert was a frontier town, and the school and jail were in the same building as the hotel. Sometimes we'd find feathers or hairpins on the floor after a dance, and we got to see criminals on their way to their cells each day. One day, when no one was around, I decided to explore the cells and accidentally locked myself in.

"Now look at the mess into which your imagination has gotten you."

144

I stomped my foot and waited for hours before I was discovered and set free.

Mr. Mustard was our headmaster. He was a bachelor who really wanted to be a minister. My stepmother invited him to visit in the evenings because she thought I might want to marry him. Can you imagine my horror? I was only fourteen!

I wrote a letter to one of my cousins:

"I heartily wish Mr. Mustard and his High School were in Venezuela."

After Mrs. Montgomery had her baby, a boy named Bruce, there were more chores assigned and I was forced to quit school. That didn't stop me from learning. I never quit reading books, and I wrote every single day. I sent one of my poems to a newspaper in Prince Edward Island.

"Good morning, Maud."

Father came to breakfast with the mail from the day before.

"May I see the paper, Father?"

Father handed me the Prince Edward Island newspaper, the *Charlottetown Patriot*. I cannot begin to tell you the way I felt when I saw my poem in print. It was the proudest day of my life, and I felt three inches taller than the day before.

"Look, Father! I've been published!" I exclaimed, shoving the paper at him.

"What?"

Father took the paper, and Mrs. Montgomery scowled.

"Oh good heavens, how many times do I have to tell you two not to read at the table?"

"Why, look here, Mary, Maud's been published. Her poem's in the paper! Well done, Maud. Well done."

Mrs. Montgomery gave a snort and left the table. My father didn't notice, since he was reading my poem, but I noticed. I always did.

Bolstered by my new status as a published author, I submitted my essay about the frontier west, entitled "A Western Eden," to the *Prince Albert Times*. It was published! Other newspapers liked the story and reprinted it. I wasn't getting paid to write, but I was getting published, and that meant everything to me.

Things at home were still difficult. My stepmother loathed the sight of me and was jealous of my relationship with my father. I missed Prince Edward Island with a constant ache that could not be healed. On New Year's Day of 1891, at a party with my two new kindred spirits, Will and Laura Pritchard, I made a wish.

"What is your wish, Maud?"

Will took my hands into his as we stared up at the stars.

"I wish to go home to Prince Edward Island," I whimpered, wiping the tears from my cheeks and laying my head on Will's shoulder.

"But I'll miss you. Are you sure you want to go?"

I nodded.

"I will miss you too, Will, but Prince Edward Island is forever

146

a part of me. You and I can still write, and I'll come back. Here," I offered, handing him my ring, "keep this by which to remember me. And when we're reunited, you can place it on my finger."

That summer, I boarded a train alone to cross Canada, to go home to my beloved island.

I didn't know that in four short years, Will would pass away. Will's sister mailed my ring back to me. I never took it off again.

CB

I wanted an education.

"An education is not going to help an ordinary Cavendish housewife. You're talking nonsense."

Grandmother didn't look up from her knitting.

"But I want to learn more. I can't bear the thought of a commonplace life."

After a year of giving music lessons and writing, I was more determined than ever to return to school to be a teacher.

"I'm going to take the teacher exam, Grandfather," I announced at supper one day.

"What on earth for?"

Grandmother dropped her fork.

"Don't worry, Grandmother, she has to pass a difficult exam to get into the college and she hasn't been to school in years," winked Grandfather, scooping up another bite of apple dumpling.

I determined to prove them wrong. I studied with the teacher

147

at the Cavendish school, took the test, and got the fifth highest score out of 264 students. My grandparents finally relented and agreed to finance my tuition at Prince of Wales College. I completed two years' worth of courses in one year to save them money and still found time to be on the staff of the school's literary magazine.

"Are you ready for exams?" mumbled my friend, Mary, who was biting her nails. "I don't know how you could study for so many at one time."

"I'm ready. You wait and see. I'm going to pass." I boasted, sounding confident, but to be honest, I was a little worried. There were two sets of exams. One was for the classes I took. The other was the teaching exam.

"Maud! Maud!" yelled my classmate, Danny, nearly running me over the day I walked into the school hall where grades were posted. "You got the highest scores in English, Drama, Literature, Agriculture, and School Management!"

I couldn't believe my ears. The crowd parted to allow me room by the postings on the wall.

"I passed!"

"You not only passed, you outdid us all," Thomas cheered.

"Mr. Harris wants to see you," Gertrude smiled. My friends pretended to hold knives at their throats. Was I in trouble?

I knocked on the office door. I could hear Mr. Harris inside.

"Come in."

I opened the door and peeked inside.

"Mr. Harris? Did you ask to see me?"

Mr. Harris stood and grinned.

"Maud, please come in. Yes, I did. Congratulations on your exams."

"Thank-you, Sir."

"I also want to congratulate you on another matter. Every year we pick the best English essay to be read at graduation. This year, your essay was chosen."

Mr. Harris handed me my essay with a first place mark on it.

"Thank-you, Sir."

I walked out of his office in a fog and into the school courtyard. I stood utterly still for a few moments and let the results of my hard work sink in deeply.

I was now a qualified teacher.

Best of all, I was an award-winning author.

After college I taught for a year in a horrible little school in Bideford. There were 48 students squeezed into one little schoolhouse, and I was their only teacher. It was not a positive experience, and I decided I preferred the life of a writer.

"I want to take some writing classes." I announced, surprising my grandparents again.

"Gracious, Maud, why can't you settle in to a regular life? I've never heard of going to school for every little thing. It's stuff and nonsense," huffed Grandmother, leaving the supper table.

I looked at my grandfather who sat packing tobacco into his pipe.

"Grandfather, I want to be a writer. There's a poet, Archibald Mechan, at Dalhouse College in Halifax who is offering a year of courses. It would be good for my writing career."

"Maud, a proper lady does not have a career."

Grandfather left the table.

I sat in silence. Was I being unreasonable? Was it terribly wrong to want to do what burned brightest in my heart?

My grandparents finally agreed and sent me to Halifax. While I was taking classes, I contracted the measles. I was still determined to get high marks and I did. I also began to sell my work. I won five dollars in an essay contest and got a check for twelve dollars for a poem published in *Youth's Companion*. My school peers grew jealous of my success.

"Oh Maud, you're awfully lucky to be published," Eli gushed over tea one stormy afternoon.

"Lucky? Do you know how many times I've been rejected? Do you know how many disappointments come to only one success? It's not all smooth sailing. The success comes only after many failures."

I don't think he believed me.

With the money I'd made, I bought five volumes of poems: Tennyson, Byron, Milton, Longfellow and Whittier.

After that year of classes, I returned to teaching for a year. My students in Belmont were as unmotivated as my students in Bideford. I boarded with a poor family in a cold farmhouse.

"What do you do up in your room early in the morning, Miss Montgomery? Why do you get up before the chickens to light the fire and warm the house?" The farmer's wife, Mrs. Leard, kept a steady rhythm as she kneaded the day's bread.

"I'm writing."

Before sunrise every morning, I sat in my room in my heaviest winter coat and boots and, with gloves on my hands in minus-twenty-nine degrees Celcius (-20 degrees Fahrenheit), I wrote.

"Writing letters?" Mrs. Leard inquired, wiping the flour off her nose.

"Um, yes, sometimes. But stories and poems mostly."

I poured myself a cup of tea and sat at the table.

"You goin' to the dance tomorrow?" Mrs. Leard smiled, as if she knew something I did not.

"I hadn't planned on it." I took a sip of the hot tea.

"I think Herman's planning on going."

She plopped the plump dough into a bowl and covered it with a towel.

I felt myself blush.

Just as I got up to leave the room, Herman, Mrs. Leard's son, came in from doing chores.

Mrs. Leard wiped her hands on her apron.

"Good morning, Herman. Miss Montgomery tells me she's not going to the dance tomorrow."

She made her way across the kitchen to fetch her broom by

the door. She nudged Herman and I cringed. Was it that obvious how much I liked him?

"Is that right? Don't you like to dance, Miss Montgomery?" winked Herman.

I grinned and stood in the doorway between the parlour and the kitchen. I looked toward the parlour window at the glistening snow.

"I love to dance. Dancing is one of my most favourite things."

"More than writing?"

Mrs. Leard grinned.

"No," I laughed and looked down at my tea, "not more than writing, but more than your homemade bread, which you know I love."

I traced the rim of my cup with my finger and looked sideways at the tall, muscular farmer's son. He was incredibly handsome, kind, and hardworking. I enjoyed our conversations at the supper table. He wasn't as intelligent as I was, but his sense of humor and friendly manner won my heart.

Herman removed his boots and sat at the kitchen table where his mother placed a large plate of potatoes and eggs.

"Have you eaten your breakfast?"

"I prefer tea in the mornings. I have a full day ahead and I had best be going."

I deposited my cup in the dishpan and ran upstairs to get my books and coat. It would be a bitterly cold walk to school this morning. When I went outside, Herman was waiting with a horse and sleigh.

"Hop in," he grinned.

I looked around.

"I suppose it would be alright. I'm not sure Grandmother would approve of my travelling alone with a man."

"You're not travelling. I'm taking you to school because it's cold."

Herman jumped off the wagon and held out his hand. I paused before allowing his giant, work-worn fingers to envelope my tiny hand and help me into the wagon.

It wasn't easy concentrating on grammar and sums. All I could think about was twirling on the dance floor with Herman Leard.

A few weeks later, a short dark-haired gentleman appeared at the back of the school room.

"Excuse me, Ma'am."

"Yes? May I help you?"

I remained at the chalkboard. The gentleman looked vaguely familiar. Was that…could it be?

"Edwin! What brings you here? Children, this is my second cousin, Edwin."

The children giggled, and Edwin blushed and gave a slight wave with the hat in his hand.

"Your grandparents told me you were here. I thought I'd come by and say hello."

"I'm finished with school in an hour. Come sit here and warm yourself."

I carried a chair and sat it beside the woodstove where Edwin sat until school was dismissed.

Afterwards, he helped me clean the chalkboard and tidy the schoolhouse. We chatted and laughed about childhood memories. It had been a long time since I'd seen Edwin.

"What did you grow up to become, Edwin?"

I pulled on my coat and gloves.

"I'm a minister."

Edwin walked with me out the backdoor.

"A minister? I'm impressed. Presbyterian, I hope."

I pushed the school door shut and locked it.

"No, Baptist."

Edwin guided me to his carriage.

"That's unfortunate," I teased.

Edwin laughed. We talked theology—one of my favourite subjects—all the way home to the Leard farm where Herman stood watching us from the barn door.

"Come inside for tea," I insisted.

Inside, Herman joined us. The men bantered back and forth about manly things. I marveled at how different the two of them were. Herman's tall, muscular frame towered over short, thin Edwin. Herman was an uneducated farm boy and Edwin a highly educated clergyman. The contrast was fascinating.

As the weeks passed, both men courted me, and I became confused. Which man would be the better husband? I enjoyed the company of them both. Herman made me laugh, and we enjoyed such fun when we were together, but he wasn't interested in intellectual things and was jealous of the time I spent writing. On the other hand, Edwin was intelligent, and our conversations were deep and meaningful. Still, there was something about Herman that I desperately loved.

"You make me laugh, Maud. I'm happiest when I'm with you," Herman confessed to me one night, as we enjoyed a warm cup of milk before bedtime.

"You make me happy, too," I smiled, looking into his rugged, sun-weathered face. His dark eyes were full of love, full of me. The way he gazed at me made me feel warm and wanted. It was odd that, though my hands shook, when I was with Herman I felt beautiful, strong, and invincible. No man had ever made me feel like that before. Even though we had little in common, in some strange way, we were kindred spirits.

"Marry me, Maud. Stop this writing nonsense and be my wife and have a family with me. I will take good care of you," he promised, reaching for my trembling hand.

My eyes filled with tears. I had no words. Give up my writing for this kind-hearted, hard-working man? Could I do it? I ran sobbing up the stairs to my room and threw myself on the bed as the kitchen door slammed below.

A week later, when Edwin was at the schoolhouse helping me clean the chalkboards, I turned around to find him on one knee.

"Maud, marry me. I will make you happy," Edwin looked up at me with such tenderness, I was crushed.

"I can't marry you, Edwin."

I sat down at my desk and held my head in my hands.

"Whatever it is, we can work it out."

Edwin remained on his knees.

"For heavens' sakes, stand up."

How exasperating! Edwin would make a wonderful husband. He loved my writing; he was proud of my success. He thought I'd make a good pastor's wife, but I wasn't so sure. Baptists don't dance and I loved to dance. But besides all that, I didn't love Edwin. He was a good friend, but I didn't love him enough to marry him.

There I was, pursued by two wonderful men: one whom I loved and could never marry, and the other who wanted to marry me, but whom I could never love.

In the midst of my courtship drama, I received a letter informing me that my grandfather had died and I was needed in Cavendish to help my grandmother. I quit my teaching job and moved home to live in the gabled house to help Grandmother, who continued to run the post office as my grandfather had.

I spent my time writing and sending my work out into the world. Nine of my manuscripts were rejected, but it didn't deter me. I knew that if I kept submitting, I would find someone who wanted to publish my writing. I learned that a lot of magazines and newspapers liked unbelievable romantic stories called "potboilers." I loathed writing them, but newspapers and magazines paid money for them and my name was becoming known.

Grandmother grew weaker, and I was needed to manage the post office a few days each week.

"How old are you now, Maud?"

Nosy Harriet Martin was famous for asking inappropriate questions.

"I'm 25 years old now, Mrs. Martin. But of course you already know that because I'm the same age as your William."

I placed the letters from her box on the counter and continued to file the mail.

"Oh, yes. It slipped my mind. Any marriage plans?"

She pretended to go through her letters. Mrs. Duncan, Mr. Conroy, and Mrs. Douglas, who stood in line behind her, leaned in for my answer.

"I've several prospects."

It wasn't entirely untrue. Herman and Edwin would take me in a heartbeat. Besides, it was none of her business.

Harriet smiled.

"That's wonderful news. I worry about you growing older up there in your grandparents' house, writing silly stories. It's not a proper life for a young woman. You need to marry and raise a family. People will think you're eccentric."

"What's wrong with being eccentric?"

I mentally ticked off the names of great writers I knew that were considered odd: Tennyson, Shakespeare, and Dickinson to name a few. If I was eccentric, I was in good company.

Harriet scowled, grabbed her mail, and left. I giggled as she slammed the door. No one else said a word.

After serving the waiting customers, I continued to sort the mail and came to a letter addressed to me. Flipping it over, I caught the name of my stepmother in the return address. That was odd. She never wrote to me. I ripped it open and sat on the stool behind the counter.

> *Dear Maud,*
> *Your father has died. I thought you'd want to know.*
> *Mrs. Montgomery*

First, my grandfather, and now my beloved father were gone. Suddenly, I felt utterly and miserably alone.

For weeks and months I mourned. I couldn't eat or sleep. I didn't have the strength or presence of mind to pick up a pen and write. I didn't write for months. It was too painful. I had wanted to become a great writer before my father died, to make him proud of me. And now, he was gone. He'd never see anything I might do.

A year later, I learned of a position as a proofreader at the newspaper, *The Daily Echo,* in Halifax, Nova Scotia. Grandmother

158

was feeling better and I needed a change. I decided to be a newspaper-woman.

"That is not a proper job for a woman," Grandmother sniffed, "not proper at all."

"And it's not proper for me to be twenty-six years old and unmarried. I can't win either way. I might as well follow my passion. I'm not doing you any good moping around here."

"I suppose you're right."

Grandmother didn't like it, but she didn't forbid me to leave either.

At the newspaper, I was the only woman on the writing staff. Other women who worked there were typists or secretaries. Women working at newspapers was considered scandalous. It wasn't ladylike to share an office with men and interview strangers.

"Maud! Get in here!" the editor yelled at me from his office at the far end of the newspaper room.

"What is it, Sir?"

I sat in the chair in front of the desk he sat behind puffing on a cigar.

"I'm going to give you a weekly column. Think you can handle that?"

He squinted at me over his glasses.

"Certainly."

I tried not to seem excited.

"I need a nice little lady column. Call it "Around the Tea

Table." You know what kind of news ladies like to read, don't you?"

He blew out a puff of smoke.

I coughed, "Yes, Sir: gossip, fashion, and society mostly."

"Good. Every Monday morning I want that column right here on my desk. You'll do this in addition to what you're already doing."

"Yes, Sir." I sat waiting as he studied the papers in front of him. He looked up.

"Well? What are you waiting for? Get busy!"

I grinned and left the office. I was a real newspaper-woman. If only Grandfather and Father could see me now.

As time went on, the editor gave me more important assignments. I wrote reviews of businesses and rewrote endings to articles other less-gifted writers had written. I was paid only $5 per week and took a part-time job helping Chinese immigrants learn English in order to pay my rent.

All my life I thought I needed perfect conditions to write, but working at the newspaper taught me that I could write in chaos. At home, I learned that I could compose stories in my head while I did housework and write them down later.

In 1902, my Grandmother fell ill again, and I quit the newspaper to care for her. Grandmother had always been strict, but in her old age she was even more difficult. I wasn't able to invite friends to visit because we could only sit in the kitchen and be quiet. I missed my exciting life as an independent newspaper-woman. It was a difficult adjustment being alone with Grandmother day after day in her house.

At least I still had my writing. In 1908 I wrote a poem called the "Island Hymn." It was published and Lawrence Watson set it to music. It became Prince Edward Island's unofficial anthem, but I wasn't able to hear it sung the first time because Grandmother was ill.

Because of my loneliness, I wrote a lot of letters and gained three pen-pals: Frank Monroe Beverly, a writer who lived in Virginia; Ephraim Weber, a Mennonite farmer in western Canada; and George Boyd MacMillan who lived in Scotland. We wrote platonic, intellectual letters and discussed many scholarly matters. Some of the letters I wrote were forty pages long and had to be delivered in a box. But my pen pals were my important friends during the lonely years of caring for my grandmother.

One day during lunch, as I was helping Grandmother with her soup, there was a light knock at our door. When I answered, a nice looking gentleman stood in the doorway.

"Hello, may I help you?"

I didn't recognize him, and I knew everyone in Cavendish from working at the post office.

"I've simply stopped by to introduce myself. I'm Rev. Ewan Macdonald."

He extended his hand.

I took his hand and shook it.

"Please, come in. My Grandmother is not well, but she will want to meet you."

I led him into the dining room.

"Grandmother, this is our new minister, Rev. Macdonald."

Grandmother looked up and tried to smile.

"I'm afraid she is too weak to speak. Would you like some tea?"

"No, thank-you. I only wanted to introduce myself. I have other homes to visit before nightfall. Are you by any chance the church organist?"

He nervously fingered the hat he held with both hands.

"Reluctantly, yes, I am. I'm not the best at it. Piano is my preferred instrument," I smiled.

He returned my smile.

"Would it be acceptable if I shared my sermon titles with you each week so that you may pick hymns accordingly?"

I liked this man's thinking.

"Certainly. It would make my job easier, I think."

I escorted him to the door.

"Perhaps you and Mrs. Macdonald would like to join us for tea sometime soon."

He blushed.

"Unfortunately there isn't yet a Mrs. Macdonald."

I felt awkward and chided myself.

"Then perhaps the Good Reverend will join us for tea very soon."

Rev. Macdonald replaced his hat with a nod.

"I shall gratefully accept such kind hospitality and will look forward to it. Good-day, Miss Montgomery."

The good Reverend was eager to share his sermon titles with me each week and began spending more and more time at the post office.

"I understand you're a very good Sunday School teacher, Miss Montgomery."

The Reverend leaned against the counter at the far end, watching me sort mail.

"I try. I've always been rather keen on theology and the Bible. It's interesting to sort it all out for young minds."

I lifted a sack of mail and untied the top.

"I'm sure you do a good job. Can I help you with that?"

He jumped over the counter and helped me sort the letters. Time passed quickly in his company and I found myself less lonely.

It didn't take the townspeople long to notice the single young minister hanging out at the post office each day. Soon rumors spread and I found that I didn't mind them.

I spent many hours with Rev. Macdonald. He was kind, intelligent, and perceptive. He was keen to debate theology and other matters. Before long, we were courting and sharing secrets with one another. But there was one secret I kept to myself, and that was the matter of writing my first book.

Besides the writing I did to my pen pals, I also wrote my own stories for our Sunday School papers. One afternoon, after seeing the picture of a red-haired little orphan girl in a magazine, a plot gradually formed in my mind about a little girl named Anne Shirley, a precocious, talkative little girl who always spoke her mind. She wasn't perfect like Anzonetta Peters. She was a girl who tried very hard to be good, but always managed to get into trouble.

I was surprised to discover that Anne Shirley's adventures refused to fit within the confines of a short story. They needed an entire book. I told no one I was writing a book, because I didn't want to be ridiculed.

I finally finished *Anne of Green Gables* in 1905 and mailed it to publishers. It was rejected many times, and I hid it away in the closet and concentrated on spending time with Rev. Macdonald.

"I would make you a good husband, Maud. You would make a good pastor's wife."

We strolled along the dirt path I had named Lover's Lane as a little girl.

"I'm not so sure I would. But I'm not getting any younger and I do want children."

I looked up at Ewan. He was smiling.

"You do many of the things pastors' wives do now, Maud. You play the organ, organize social events, teach Sunday School. Our little church would be lost without your influence."

He squeezed my hand.

"When do you leave for sabbatical?"

I would miss him while he was away in Scotland.

"In another week. I have much to do before leaving, but all I want is to be with you." Ewan stopped walking and turned me toward him, placing his hands on my shoulders.

"Will you think about saying yes, if I were to propose to you before I left?"

I looked into his eyes. The kind of love I saw wasn't the same as I'd seen in Herman's. But there was trust and warmth and kindness. At the age of 32, I no longer hoped for true love, but I longed for the stability and security of marriage. I wanted children and a family of my own. Could this man give me those things?

"I'll think and pray hard about it, Ewan."

I held his hands to my cheek.

He wrapped me in his arms.

"That's all I ask."

Before he left in October, 1906, Ewan gave me a ring and asked me again to marry him.

I said yes.

Married Maud

Five years passed before Ewan and I could marry. Two years after the proposal, my first book, *Anne of Green Gables,* was published.

"Ewan! Look! My book has arrived new from the publishers! Isn't it lovely?"

I tenderly ran my hands across the ecru cloth stamped in gold letters and touched the illustration of Anne pasted on the cloth case. I was awestruck to see my words in print and my name on the front of a book.

"It is indeed," Ewan agreed. "I'm proud of you, Maud, real proud."

In those five years before my marriage, I finished two more books, *Anne of Avonlea* and *Kilmeny of the Orchard.* I was getting paid to write, and my name was being recognized.

As I sorted the mail one day, Ewan let out a grunt while reading a newspaper.

"What is it? Did something bite you?"

I walked to where he stood beside the counter.

"Did you read this?"

He held out the *Charlottetown Patriot* newspaper.

I shook my head.

"No, I haven't the chance. You're always snatching it from my hands as soon as it arrives."

"Read it!"

He pointed to an article on the second page.

"Congratulations to our own Prince Edward Island author, L. M. Montgomery, for garnering the praise of Mark Twain himself who stated in a letter to Francis Wilson: "In Anne of Green Gables you will find the dearest and most moving and delightful child since the immortal Alice." This is quite something coming

from the best-selling author who created Huckleberry
Finn and Tom Sawyer. Well done to our Prince Edward
Island darling!"

I looked up and grinned and then stared down at the article again.

"I only wish Father could have read this."

Ewan placed his hand over mine.

"He probably knows, Maud, don't you think? If souls are happy in heaven, then I think he knows."

In 1910, I travelled to Boston to meet my publishers. Even though I was shy, I relished the excuse to wear pretty clothes and eat fancy food. I bought my first real evening dress for one of the galas.

One night after a high society dinner, I looked up at the stars and with my imagination tried to comprehend that they were the same stars that shone over Cavendish. When I looked a little longer at the moon, I realized with even greater fascination that it was a lunar eclipse.

"What do you see, Miss Montgomery?"

A lady dressed in sequins and feathers giggled at my odd behavior. I stood surrounded by wealth, expensive, shimmering gowns, and fancy tuxedos, but I stood in the street staring at the sky.

"It's a lunar eclipse. See there?"

I pointed to the moon.

"God writes the most spectacular stories, if you'll take the time to notice."

On March 10, 1911, Grandmother Macneill passed away. Because it wasn't proper for a woman to live alone, I was forced to move into my Uncle John's house, and Ewan and I decided to make plans for our marriage.

We had a quiet, intimate wedding in my uncle's house on July 5, 1911. It was considered improper to have a lavish wedding when one was in mourning.

"You look lovely, Maud," cried my aunt as she wrapped me in her arms.

I looked down at my beautiful dress made of ivory silk crepe with touches of chiffon and jewels. I was 37 years old and finally going to have a family of my own. There was a knock on the bedroom door. My aunt answered it and someone handed her a jewel box.

"This is for you from Ewan," she spoke softly, as if it was something sacred.

I opened the box to find a beautiful amethyst necklace.

I gasped, "Oh, amethysts! He remembered. Will you help me put it on? I want to wear it now."

My aunt helped me with the necklace, and I looked at myself in the mirror. I was no longer young. I was now a mature, independent woman. I wiped away a tear.

Aunt Annie handed me my bouquet of white roses, lily of the valley, and ferns. Alone, I made my way to the parlour to meet my groom. After a short ceremony and a gentle kiss, I became Mrs. Ewan Macdonald.

Maud's Golden Years

"Ewan, would you like a cup of tea?"

Ewan sat in a chair staring out the window. It had been several days since he'd spoken. The severe depression that plagued him our entire marriage seemed to have swallowed him whole, but I still tried to reach him.

"It's a lovely day for a stroll, don't you think?"

I walked to the Victrola and started a Cole Porter recording.

"Should I dance for you, Ewan? Will that cheer you?"

He didn't respond, but I had plenty of words to fill all the empty spaces.

"Ewan, do you remember how Mrs. Maloney caught me listening to the Victrola when we first moved into the manse in Leaksdale, and how upset you were? You thought you were going to be fired."

I danced around the room, looking for a glimmer of recognition. Ewan was no longer a pastor, and I was free of my constant duties as a pastor's wife: attending weddings, baptisms and funerals, hosting teas. I can't say I missed it. The constant covering up for Ewan's depression and hiding it from church members took its toll on me and our boys.

"Do you remember how I'd get up early in the morning and write before you and the boys awoke?"

I wiped the spittle from Ewan's chin and whispered in his ear.

"Ewan, I know you're in there. I know you can hear me.

Tell me to stop talking like you used to. Tell me to bring you your slippers."

There was no answer. I sat across from Ewan in my chair by the window and recalled the life we'd shared. In 1912 the *Chronicles of Avonlea* was published and my first son, Chester Cameron, was born. I lost one baby after him, and in October 1915 my son, Ewan Stuart (we called him Stuart), arrived.

"I don't know how I did it in those days, Ewan."

I reached over and took his hand. Why could I remember everything and Ewan could remember so little? It wasn't fair.

In 1915, in the midst of two babies and being a pastor's wife, *Anne of the Island* was published. In 1917, my half brother, Carl, moved in with us. He had been wounded in the Battle of Vimy Ridge and lost his leg after lying in the snow for eighteen hours.

"Oh, Ewan. You were the only one in my life to whom I could turn and yet you couldn't understand."

I reached over and brushed the hair out of his eyes.

"No one knew how I suffered with no one in whom to confide. How lonely I was! How I missed my island. How hard I worked to keep you sane and your position as a pastor. I have always been utterly alone in this world."

At least I had my books.

I stared up at the bookshelf where my titles sat like trophies, including the 1917 first edition of *Anne's House of Dreams* and the 1919 edition of *Rainbow Valley*.

170

I glanced over at the mantel and smiled at my Royal Society of Arts of England commendation and my Silver Medal of Literary Style from France. Those were the true golden years of knowing I had made an impression on this world.

On the table lay my latest two books, *Anne of Windy Poplars* and *Anne of Ingleside*. Each day I read to Ewan from one of them, hoping he would recognize my voice and come back to me.

"Ewan, I'm tired and my headaches come more often now. I'm too tired to lift my pen again. I think I'll just sit here and close my eyes one last time.

"And dream of my beautiful island."

Author's Notes:

Lucy Maude Montgomery determined to make a living as a writer at a time when very few women could. During her lifetime she wrote twenty novels and more than five hundred short stories, poems, and essays. Her books were published in Japanese, Icelandic, Polish, Finnish, Swedish, and Braille. Japanese children are especially fond of *Anne of Green Gables* and grow up with the dream of being married on Prince Edward Island.

Anne's stories are included in the Japanese school reading curriculum. She appeals to the Japanese because she must work hard to please her elders and she places a high value on education. Japanese vacationers are some of Prince Edward Island's most enthusiastic tourists.

On May 7, 2010, the Legislative Assembly of Prince Edward Island finally adopted "The Island Hymn" as the official provincial anthem of Prince Edward Island.

After nearly a century, her books are still read and loved by people young and old all over the world. *Anne of Green Gables* was one of the Duchess of Cambridge's (Kathryn Middleton's) favourite childhood books. The newly married Duchess visited Prince Edward Island with her new husband, Prince William, during their tour of Canada on July 3- 4, 2011.

L.M. Montgomery's Novels

1908 - Anne of Green Gables

1909 - Anne of Avonlea

1910 - Kilmeny of the Orchard

1911 - The Story Girl

1913 - The Golden Road

1915 - Anne of the Island

1917 - Anne's House of Dreams

1919 - Rainbow Valley

1920 - Rilla of Ingleside

1923 - Emily of New Moon

1925 - Emily Climbs

1926 - The Blue Castle

1927 - Emily's Quest

1929 - Magic for Marigold

1931 - A Tangled Web

1933 - Pat of Silver Bush

1935 - Mistress Pat

1936 - Anne of Windy Poplars

1937 - Jane of Lantern Hill

1939 - Anne of Ingleside

THE DISCOVERY OF INSULIN BY SIR FREDERICK GRANT BANTING, KBE, MC, FRSC[i]
NOVEMBER 14, 1891 - FEBRUARY 21, 1941

Seven-year-old Fred lay in the dark, worrying about the bear under his bed.

"Mr. Bear, if you don't bother me, I won't bother you." He whispered into the shadows of the small farmhouse bedroom, quietly wondering if he would hear the bear stir. Although he had never seen a bear on his farm in Alliston, Ontario, he heard there were bears living in the woods nearby.

"If there was really a bear under my bed, the bear would bite my face. Wouldn't you bite me, Mr. Bear?"

---

[i]KBE: Knight Commander of the Order of the British Empire; MC: Military Cross; FRSC: Fellow of the Royal Society of Canada

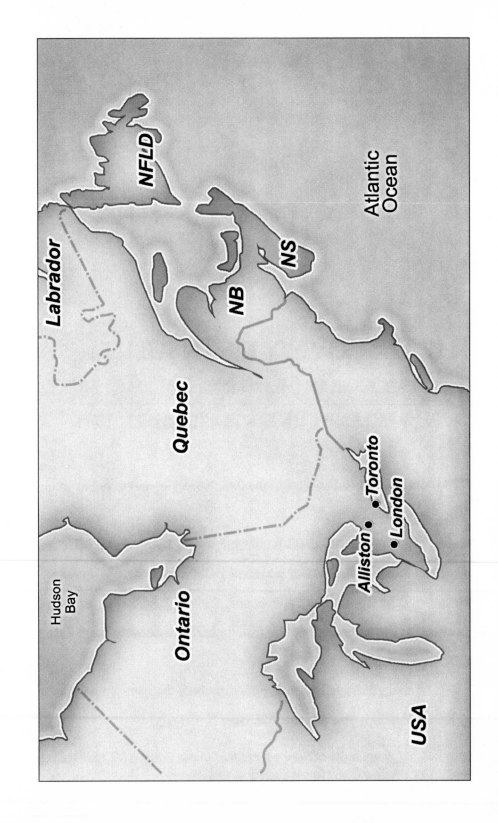

He received no answer.

Fred lay still in the darkness a little longer, unable to sleep at the thought of the giant beast hibernating under his bed.

"Maybe the bear is sleeping. But if he were asleep, I would hear him snore, wouldn't I?"

Fred sat up in the dark and gave it more thought. Mother had blown out the kerosene lamps. There was no light to see by. If there was a bear under his bed, he would have to find out by feeling around for him in the dark.

"If I can't see him, he can't see me."

Emboldened by his logic, Fred jumped to the floor and reached frantically under the bed.

There was no bear. He crawled back into bed and fell into a sound sleep.

The next morning at breakfast Fred had an announcement to make, "There is no bear under my bed, Kenneth. I don't care what you say. You can't fool me."

"Kenneth, did you tell your little brother there was a bear under his bed?"

Mother scolded Kenneth as she set a plate of pancakes in front of Fred.

Thirteen-year-old Kenneth tried to hide his grin, "Maybe."

"No wonder I've been having trouble getting him to bed at night. No seconds for you."

Mother removed Kenneth's plate and poured Father another

cup of coffee. Fred's two older brothers, Nelson and Thompson, were already at work on their own farm-fields.

"You're a very brave young man, Fred, to go hunting that bear all alone. Now, eat your breakfast. Mama, hand me my Bible. It's getting late."

Father pointed to the big clock on the shelf behind the kitchen table.

Mama handed Papa the Bible and he read from Proverbs 12:10: "'A righteous man regardeth the life of his beast: but the tender mercies of the wicked are cruel.' What do you think that means?"

Essie, Fred's ten-year-old sister, raised her hand as if she were in school.

"I know. I think it means that wise people take good care of their animals and that cruel people don't."

Father smiled.

"Very good, Essie; you're exactly right. We have a responsibility to the animals we raise. Even if we raise them for food, we are to make sure they are comfortable and well cared for."

"That's why the animals follow Papa all over the farm," Mama smiled, "the cat, the dog…"

Fred swung his feet and grinned.

"The lambs and the piglets."

Essie hugged Father and hung on his arm.

"They all love Father because he is kind."

"Your Papa is a good example. All the animals trust him and

178

we can trust him to take care of us just as the Heavenly Father takes care of us," Mother smiled.

Father shut the Bible.

"It's time to pray now. Bow your heads."

After prayers Father hitched up their Clydesdale horse, Old Sue, to the plough and little Fred rode high on her back. That summer he grew tawny and muscular as he helped in the fields on the farm. He also helped his sister gather eggs, feed the chickens, and bring in the cows.

"Would you and Essie like to help me pick huckleberries today, Fred?"

Mama took her berry basket off the hook by the kitchen door.

"Will you make me a pie?"

Fred loved his mother's pies.

"It depends on how many huckleberries we manage to bring home. You usually eat more than you pick."

Mama handed Fred his own basket and tied on her bonnet. Fred pulled on his straw hat and followed Mama and Essie to the berry patch.

Fred and Essie spent most of the afternoon picking berries and chasing butterflies. Before Fred managed to pick enough to fill his basket, clouds rolled in above them and a thunderstorm threatened to push aside the sunny day.

"We best be going, Fred. Where's Essie?" Mother asked as she craned her neck to see.

Fred pointed a purple-stained hand toward his sister.

"She's over there, by that bunch of bushes by the fence row."

"Fetch your sister and come on home. I'm going to run ahead and get supper started. Don't dawdle. The storm won't wait much longer."

Mother headed on down the trail toward home and Fred went back to get Essie.

"Essie! Time to go home! Essie! Where are you?"

Fred looked behind the huckleberry bush by the fence row but didn't find his sister there.

"I'm over here!" Essie called to him from the line of trees at the edge of the woods.

"What are you doing over there?" Fred yelled as he ran towards the sound of her voice.

"Look what I found!"

Essie stood up from where she had squatted and held up an arrowhead.

"There are all sorts of them. Here, you can have this one. Help me look for more."

Fred forgot all about the impending storm as he and Essie searched and filled their pockets full of arrow and spear heads.

Thunder rumbled.

"The storm! Essie, c'mon; we gotta hurry and get home. Mama said."

"You don't have to tell me twice. I hate thunder," shivered

180

Essie, grabbing Fred's hand as they ran several miles to the farmhouse, across two fields and a country trail.

Halfway home they came to the Alliston family cemetery. The wind increased and blew leaves and sticks up and over graves and into their path. Fred was a brave boy, but his sister's imagination could get the best of him.

"I hope there aren't any ghosts haunting in the storm," whispered Essie as she gripped Fred's hand tighter.

"There ain't no such thing as ghosts, Essie. Mama said so. You're hurting my hand."

Fred tried to pull away but Essie's grip tightened.

"We can get home faster if we walk through the cemetery," Essie hollered above the sound of the wind. Her skirts whipped around her legs as she held her straw hat with one hand and held tightly onto Fred with the other. The basket of huckleberries swung back and forth on her arm, spilling most of its contents as they ran.

"What about the ghosts?" Fred hollered back.

"You said there weren't any ghosts, remember? C'mon." Essie pulled Fred through the cemetery, tripping over fallen limbs and vines. Fred shielded his face from the blowing leaves and dust.

As they made their way across the graveyard, a large white figure approached from behind the Alliston family mausoleum.

"A ghost!" Essie screamed and ran faster, dragging little Fred behind her.

"Essie, Essie, stop! Stop! It's not a ghost! Stop, Essie, you're hurting me!" Fred screamed, breaking free from her grasp. "Essie, it's not a ghost!"

Fred watched Essie disappear into the rain and then turned back toward the figure moving among the tombstones.

"You're no ghost. You're Mrs. McKnight's Jersey cow. C'mon girl, I'll take you home until after the storm."

Fred leaned against the wind and led the old cow home in the downpour. He locked her safely inside the family barn and headed towards the house.

"Where have you been?" Mother asked as she pushed the huckleberry pie into the oven and shut the door.

"Chasing ghosts with Essie," Fred grinned. He was four years younger than Essie, but today he was the bigger boy.

⅓

Every Sunday, Fred's family attended services at the Alliston Wesley Methodist Church. Today there would be a Sunday School picnic following services. Fred's mouth watered all through church, imagining Mrs. Brandt's Maple Sugar Pie and Mr. McCullough's homemade peach ice cream.

Fred had a difficult time listening in Sunday School.

"Fred? Did you hear what I said?" Mrs. Martindale tapped the table in front of him.

"Uh, I'm sorry, Mrs. Martindale."

Fred tugged at his stiffly starched shirt collar. It made his neck itch.

"I asked if you studied your lesson. Do you know your memory verse?"

Mrs. Martindale was a stickler for memory verses.

Fred shook his head and sheepishly replied, "No, Mrs. Martindale. I can't remember it."

"Did you practice it at all?" Mrs. Martindale's voice sounded disappointed. Fred wanted to please his kind teacher.

"Yes, but no matter how many times I try to remember, I don't," Fred frowned.

Mrs. Martindale patted his hand. "You'll do better next week, I'm sure."

During the sermon, the smell of fried chicken and sugar-baked ham filled the air. Fred's tummy rumbled, thinking of all the goodies that waited for him after the service.

"Sit still, Fred, and listen." Mama pinched his ear. Fred rubbed the soreness away. He was listening. A boy could imagine ice cream and Jesus with the five loaves and fishes all at once, couldn't he?

After worship, Fred helped the men set out the saw horses and top them with wooden planks and old doors to make tables. He helped carry the church benches outside and onto the lawn, while girls dressed in their Sunday-best covered the make-shift tables with crisp white tablecloths.

Standing in line, Fred could hardly wait, hoping there would still be ice cream left for him by the time he reached the end.

"Put your silverware in your pocket, Fred, so you don't lose it and be sure to put it back in the basket when you're done." Mama handed him a spoon and fork. Fred tucked them into the front pocket of his shirt and he hopped on one foot and then the next, as he waited in line. The delicious smells of fresh bread, pickles, and country ham tickled his nose and made the wait more difficult. Mrs. Martindale entertained the diners with her fiddle playing, and Fred was thankful at that moment that he did not know how to play the fiddle because he would be last in line for ice cream.

Fred piled his plate high with all his favorites, including his mother's potato salad and a generous slice of huckleberry pie.

"Come sit here by me, Fred," Mary Jane hollered loud enough for all the boys in his Sunday School class to hear.

"Come sit here by me, Fred," Harry mocked, and Fred's face grew hot. He avoided all of them and sat under a tree by himself. He was too shy to sit by the other children, and there was no more room by his parents at the table.

Fred's stomach was nearly bursting when Gerald recruited him for a game of catch. The boys tossed a ball back and forth several times before it landed in Mrs. Peabody's strawberry jam.

"Fred, take that out to the field!" his father scolded.

"Yes, Father!" Fred bellowed, tossing the ball back and forth from hand to hand and walking backwards. He cut behind a tree without seeing Mrs. Martindale's violin resting against it.

Crack!

Zing!

184

Fred heard the violin under his foot and was too afraid to look down. He turned and ran away.

The next morning at breakfast, Fred couldn't eat. His stomach was in knots and the table looked like it was moving.

"What's wrong, Fred, are you sick?"

His mother felt his forehead.

"I don't feel well," Fred groaned and put his head on the table.

"Go back to bed," ordered his mother as she helped him to the stairs, "I'll be up to check on you later."

Fred sat in his room and stared out the window. How could he tell his parents he broke Mrs. Martindale's violin? He was sure it must cost more than a house. He would have to work forever to pay for it.

Day after day, Fred did his best to push the broken violin from his mind. He kept himself busy hunting for arrowheads. He went swimming in the river and built a dog house for his dog, Jap. There were no friends nearby with whom to play, so he took long walks in the woods and talked to the animals on the farm.

"Dear God, could you please let Sunday never come? And Lord, if you can heal a blind man, you can heal a violin, now can't you? If Sunday has to come, can you please heal Mrs. Martindale's violin?"

No matter how much Fred prayed for it not to, Sunday arrived right on schedule.

"Fred, time for breakfast! Where are you?" His mother looked all through the upstairs. Fred could not be found.

"I saw him outside early this morning doing his chores" Kenneth sat down at the table and poured himself a tall glass of milk.

"What has gotten into that boy?" His mother sighed and shook her head. "He's acted strange all week."

"Maybe he's nervous about going to school," Father sat down and sipped his coffee.

The family arrived at church together in the family wagon. Fred slipped around to the back of the church and avoided going inside. He feared to look Mrs. Martindale in the eye, knowing he had destroyed her precious violin.

After Sunday School, Fred slipped into the pew beside his parents while the choir sang the first song.

"Where have you been?" Essie hissed and pointed to his shirt. "Tuck that in."

Fred tucked in his shirt and reached for a hymnal under the pew in front of him. Just as he opened its pages the beautiful strains of a violin reached his ears. He peeked up over the pew and saw Mrs. Martindale, more beautiful than ever, playing a fully intact instrument.

Fred stood up straight and joined the congregation's refrain of *"Hosanna Loud Hosanna"* louder than he'd ever sung before.

"Hosanna, loud hosanna,
The little children sang,
Through pillared court and temple

The lovely anthem rang.
To Jesus, who had blessed them
Close folded to his breast,
The children sang their praises,
The simplest and the best. "

In the wagon on the way home from church, Mama leaned over to talk in Papa's ear, "Did you hear little Fred singing at the top of his lungs this morning? I don't know what's gotten into that boy. I just don't know what's gotten into him."

ೞ

It was Fred's first day of school, and the shy boy wanted nothing of it. The walk from his home to the town of Alliston was long and boring, and there were not many country boys his age attending school.

Schoolwork was hard for Fred. He had a difficult time learning to read, and spelling was even more arduous. He often flipped letters or left them out completely. But as much as he hated class time, lunch was worse.

For an hour and a half, Fred was alone for lunch. The town children went home to a hot meal and playtime with friends. Fred was left alone. Often he was too upset to eat and threw his lunch in the river or gave it to the Mayburys' dog.

On his birthday, Fred decided to go to the old fair grounds to eat his lunch.

"I will not cry today. If I don't cry today I won't cry any other day because what happens on my birthday will happen the rest of the year."

The harder Fred tried not to cry, the more he cried. And he cried every other day of the year just as he predicted.

"What are you crying about, crybaby?" the kids at school teased him, making him cry all the more.

After school each day, he ran home and threw his arms around his beloved dog, Jap.

"Oh, Jap, I hate school. Even if I know an answer to the question, I'm too afraid to say it. I can't spell: every word has three ways of spelling it, and I always guess wrong. And I have no friends. No friends in the world but you."

As Fred grew older, he became more and more quiet and shy. When his distant cousin, Marion Walwyn, met him for the first time, they sat together in the swing in the yard for over an hour and never said a word.

Night after night, Fred worked on his spelling. He wrote the words ten times each, but always got low marks on all his papers because he could not spell. The only time Fred felt happy was when he worked on the farm, caring for the animals, healing them, and keeping them comfortable.

When Fred was twelve, he needed new boots for school. All of Fred's clothes were handed down to him from his older siblings. Fred never minded, because clothes weren't anything about which he ever

188

worried–until his mother gave him his sister's old high button boots.

Essie had outgrown them quickly and the sturdy boots had been hardly worn.

Mother handed the boots to Fred.

"These boots are practically brand new and of excellent quality. These will do for you for school this year, Fred."

Fred was horrified. Girls' boots had small high heels and they buttoned up on each side. Boys' boots looked nothing like them. He was already picked on at school. What would the mean boys do to him now?

Every day on his way to school, Fred took off the boots and hid them under the bridge over the Boyne River. Each day he hated them more. Before taking them off he'd kick every stone and dunk them in water to make them old. He ground the bottoms with rocks but no matter what he did, the boots would not wear out.

The weather grew colder, but Fred refused to wear the boots to school. Finally, when snow was on the ground, he had no choice. He had to wear them.

He arrived at school from the back fields and waited outside in the yard. As soon as the bell rang, he ran to his desk and tucked his feet far underneath it. The entire morning, instead of concentrating on his school work, he worried about recess.

Fred had good reason to worry. As soon as he bolted for the door, the class bully, "Smack" Golden, caught sight of Fred's boots.

"Look at the little sissy-girl, wearing Mother's boots."

The boys chased Fred into the yard, taunting him. Fred started to run away, but when the taunts grew louder, something in him snapped.

He turned to face the giant.

And when Smack hit Fred, the normally quiet little boy fought back.

"Fight!"

A circle formed around the two boys, and Fred stood up to the other boy. Smack was a smoker and didn't have the strength of Fred.

"Stop! Stop!" Smack covered his face with his hands to hide the stains of tears as he lay down on the ground.

Fred almost liked the boots then. They had helped him find courage he did not know he possessed, and he gained a few friends too.

A few days later, when walking with his mother down the street, Fred walked close to his mother's skirts to hide the boots.

"Fred, what on earth are you doing?" His mother glared.

Fred looked down and confessed, "I'm ashamed of wearing my sister's boots."

Fred's mother was shocked. She never imagined the pain she had caused by asking Fred to wear girls' boots.

"My dear child, why didn't you tell me? Let's go buy a pair of boots fit for a boy."

As time went by, Fred only grew more shy and stubborn. He got picked on at recess, left alone at lunch time, and was in constant

190

trouble with his teacher for not being able to answer questions correctly.

"Fred, please come to the board and distinguish between the nominative absolute and the noun or pronoun modified by a participle that is used as subject or object of a verb in the sentence I've written on the board."

The teacher held out the piece of chalk in her hand.

Fred felt hot. His palms were clammy. No matter how many times he read the sentence on the board, he could not understand what the teacher was asking him to do. He went to the board and read the sentence over and over again.

He having finished the work, we were not obliged to remain.

Fred hung his head in shame. He could not do it. He did not know where to start.

"I...I don't know how to do this," Fred stammered, handing the chalk back to the teacher. His classmates snickered as he went back to his desk.

"Frederick Banting, you should be ashamed of yourself for not paying attention in class. If you would pay attention, you wouldn't have trouble with your studies. I bet Willie Morrison can diagram this sentence. Willie, come here and show Fred how it's done."

Willie went to the board and diagrammed the sentence with no trouble at all.

It still did not make sense to Fred.

"See, Fred? You need to quit acting stupid and pay attention.

You're always dreaming. You have no focus."

Fred looked out the window as the teacher continued to insult him in front of his classmates. He grew angrier with every word she spoke. When the bell rang for lunch, he went straight home and vowed never to return to school again.

"What are you doing home?" Mother stood by the sink skimming milk, as Fred walked in the door and set his books on the table.

"I'm never going back to school as long as I live."

"Nonsense, of course you will." Mother poured a glass of fresh milk and handed it to Fred. She poured the cream she had skimmed off the top into a butter churn jar for making butter later.

Father walked into the room. He'd overheard the conversation from the dining room.

"No, Mother, I think that's fine. We need an extra man around here and there's plenty of work. If Fred wants to be a labourer, there's nothing wrong with that. Think it over, Fred, and while you're thinking, put on your overalls and clean out the hen house."

Fred did not know what was worse: cleaning out the hen house or being humiliated at school. He decided nothing could be as distasteful as cleaning that stinky chicken coop and the next day went back to class. But Fred did such a good job of cleaning the hen house, his father gave him the responsibility of cleaning it every Saturday morning. It was a weekend reminder of Fred's future, should he decide to quit school.

192

Most farm boys and girls in those days didn't go to high school. Many quit going to school by grade six or grade eight. For Fred to decide to attend high school, when the work was such a challenge for him, was admirable.

When the Banting boys reached the age of twenty-one, they were each given the gift of $1500, a horse, and a buggy. They could use the money to start their own farm or go to college. Fred decided to go to college.

His mother and father thought Fred would grow up to be a minister, but Fred had other aspirations. It came to him one day on his way home from school, while watching men shingle a roof. As he studied their movements, a scaffolding broke, causing two men to fall. They were badly hurt, and Fred ran to fetch the doctor.

As Fred watched the doctor at work, he marveled at the doctor's ability to tend to the men's cuts and broken bones. In those short moments, his fate was sealed: he would become a doctor.

Fred went away to college in Toronto and received nominal grades, until he began taking classes in medicine. It was in these classes that he excelled. Spelling didn't matter as much, and Fred proved himself a fine surgeon. He had skilled hands from growing up working on the farm.

Every Sunday Fred wrote to his mother and continued this habit for the rest of his life. Sometimes on weekends, Fred desired to visit his home. His sister, Essie, drove the carriage with Fred's horse,

Mollie, and parked the horse in the church shed. Fred would call the horse's name as he drew near.

"Where are you, Mollie?"

The horse whinnied in excited anticipation of seeing her beloved master. Fred hugged her neck and spoke gently to the horse.

"You know my voice, don't you, Mollie? I'll always know yours, too, old girl."

Mollie answered in soft whinnies.

In one of his college notebooks Fred Banting wrote,

> *"She could almost talk. I shall always remember the conversations that we had on those nights when I returned from college and hugged her all over and how she talked back."*

On August 15, 1914, one day after the British Empire declared war on Germany, Fred tried to join the army, but he was rejected for poor eyesight. After his third year in medical school, he tried to enlist again and was accepted. The army promoted him to sergeant in the Canadian Army Medical Service.

He spent his last years of medical school taking classes in the day and caring for wounded soldiers at night. When he performed his first operation, Fred sat with the soldier the entire night, frightened that he would bleed to death. Forty-eight hours after Fred lanced an abscess on the sick soldier's tonsils, the infantryman rejoined his battalion to deploy overseas.

An oil painting of Sir Frederick Banting in 1925 by Tibor Polya,
now in the possession of the National Portrait Gallery of Canada

On one of his visits home, Fred fell in love with the minister's

daughter, Edith Roach. The attractive couple caused a stir when they

went to church together. Fred looked rugged and handsome in his

soldier's uniform, and Edith was an attractive, popular young woman.

Before being sent to Europe for the Great War, he asked

Edith to marry him and gave her a diamond ring. She said yes, but

they never married. Many years later, in 1924, Fred married Marion

Robertson and they had one child, William, in 1928. Unfortunately,

this marriage ended in divorce in 1932. Banting went on to marry

Henrietta Ball in 1937.

On August 8, 1918, "the black day of the German army,"

Canadian forces attacked east of Amiens, France. Fred worked on the

front lines, receiving the wounded and cleaning, closing, and dressing their many wounds. On September 2, Fred wrote in his war-diary:

> *"The barrages were terrific on both sides. I went over the top with the battalion. We passed through heavy shell-fire and gas volley…The wounded poured in and I kept eighteen bearers and twenty to thirty Huns carrying out. A couple of nice Heinies worked around all day…I got a little sleep during the night but had to wear a gas mask for about four hours."*

Fred was fearless. When wounded men fell, he ran with stretcher-bearers to retrieve them and take them to the aid post. He worked tirelessly through the nights. When the men who went with him were wounded, he stopped in the midst of gunfire to attend them.

Once, while attending the wounded in the midst of a battle, he watched as soldiers of the British cavalry galloped on horseback into the fray. They soon retreated due to heavy German fire. When a shell exploded near the commander and his horse, the horse got to its feet and started galloping away. Then it stopped, ran back to its master, and in the midst of gunfire allowed the commander to mount. Fred was overwhelmed and fascinated by the intelligence, discipline, and bravery of the animal as it dodged bullets and delivered its soldier to safety.

An hour later, Fred was wounded by shrapnel from an exploding shell. He wanted to stay on the front lines, but his friend, Palmer, insisted he be treated for his wounds. For his courage, Fred was awarded the Military Cross:

"[When] Capt. Frederick Grant Banting... medical officer of the 46th Canadian Battalion was wounded, he immediately proceeded forward through intense shell fire to reach the battalion. Several of his men were wounded and he, neglecting his own safety, stopped to attend to them. While doing this he was wounded himself and was sent out notwithstanding his plea to be left at the front. His energy and pluck were of a very high order."

Fred's arm did not heal quickly. He spent nine weeks in hospital due to infection. Three weeks after the war ended, in February 1919, he was released from the hospital and stationed in Toronto, Canada to help mend the broken bodies of wounded Canadian soldiers.

Fred was no longer the scared little boy who cried every day at school. He was a strong, bold, and courageous young man. The war had helped him to grow up.

After the war, he moved to London, Ontario, and opened his own private practice, but he never had enough to do and became bored. One day in late July 1920, he passed by a store and spotted a painting.

"I could paint a picture," Fred told himself. He walked into the store and bought the picture and some paint. That is when he began to paint pictures he saw in magazines and books. He also wrote stories and filled his notebooks with poems and narratives.

One night in November, after Fred had spent the day preparing for a lecture he was to give on the pancreas and diabetes, he couldn't sleep. He began to think about how to obtain the secretions from the inside of the pancreas and wrote down an idea in his notebook:

> *"Ligate pancreatic* ducts of dogs…Try to isolate the internal secretion…"

Early in 1921, Fred Banting took his idea to Professor John Macleod, who was a leading figure in the study of diabetes in Canada.

"I don't think your idea has much merit, Banting. Stick to your doctoring," Macleod grumbled without looking up from his work.

"What do you have to lose, Macleod--a few dogs? It would cost very little to try."

Macleod didn't think Banting's idea would work, but he gave Banting a small, primitive laboratory space and a few dogs at the University of Toronto. Banting recruited medical student, Charles Best, to help him, and they began their experiments in the summer of 1921.

It bothered Fred to experiment on dogs. He loved animals, and it pained him to see them suffer and die. But watching people suffer from diabetes was also painful. Dr. Banting treated the dogs with utmost care and respect, as his father had taught him.

On one set of dogs, they performed surgery by tying off

their pancreatic ducts in order to stop the flow of nourishment to the pancreas, causing it to shrink. After a while, they removed the pancreases completely, sliced them up, and froze the pieces in a mixture of water and salts. When the pieces were half-frozen, they were ground up and filtered. The isolated substance was named "isletin."

Another set of dogs had their pancreas removed completely. Without pancreases the dogs became diabetic: their blood sugars rose, they drank lots of water and urinated more often, and became weaker and weaker.

The "isletin" was injected into the diabetic dogs. Their blood glucose levels dropped, and they seemed healthier and stronger. By giving the diabetic dogs a few injections a day, Banting and Best could keep them healthy and free of symptoms. But more tests needed to be done to prove to Macleod that they had discovered a way to treat diabetes.

More tests meant they needed more pancreases. One day, Banting walked past a cattle slaughterhouse and got the idea of using the pancreases of cattle. They tried this idea, and when they injected the sick dogs with the "isletin" from the cow pancreases, to their delight, the dogs got better.

That summer in Toronto was hot, humid, and miserable. The work in the lab was exhausting. Banting cut the sleeves off his lab coat and pants. He even cut the pant legs off his pajamas so he could sleep at night. Sweat rolled off Banting's arms and forehead during the surgeries, infecting some of the dogs and causing them to die. It was frustrating work.

In the middle of a hot summer, the offensive smell of so many dogs in one place was also overwhelming. Banting was hot, irritated, and impatient. When he saw the dirty beakers Best had carelessly left in the lab, he blew up.

"Best! We won't have good data if you're using dirty glass. You've got to clean up, man! These beakers and this equipment – they must be kept clean! Do you understand me?"

Best was unaccustomed to seeing Banting act this way. He set to work right away cleaning up the mess and from then on, the lab was spotless.

One of the dogs, named Dog 92, was Dr. Banting's favourite. She was a yellow collie who was sweet and frisky.

"Hey there, 92, how are ya?" Dr. Banting scratched the happy dog behind the ears.

"She's a great dog, Fred," Best knelt down beside the dog and stroked her long coat.

"It's a shame to make her sick," Fred sighed. "Old girl, I wish we didn't have to do it, but you're helping mankind."

Dog 92 licked Fred's face and hands before falling asleep on the operating table.

After her pancreas was removed she became extremely ill from diabetes, and Dr. Banting injected her with "isletin." At first, the dog got well and became active and happy.

"Look at you! You're a feisty girl today!" Dr. Banting greeted his favorite dog and scratched behind her ears. She did not appear sick at all.

The doctor repeated the same experiment on cats, but it failed. And eventually, beloved Dog 92 became ill and died.

The brave young doctor, who had dodged shells and bullets in the Great War, wept bitterly over the loss of his dear pet. Watching the dogs suffer took its toll on the heroic doctor. He hated doing what he had to do, but he was having more success with the cattle pancreases. He showed the results to Macleod, who was convinced Dr. Banting was making important discoveries.

"I like what I see here in your data, Banting," smiled Macleod. "I'm going to move you to a better lab and advance you more funds."

"Thank-you, Professor, I can't tell you how much this means to me." Banting was delighted.

"No thanks needed. This work is important. I also think you should name the extract "insulin" – just a suggestion. This new lab I'm going to give you is bigger and has better working conditions. You'll have more room for the dogs, and it'll be easier to care for them. Keep up the good work."

Macleod had a new excitement and passion for Dr. Banting's work and, in December 1921, asked biochemist J.B. Collip to join the team to help them purify the formula. It wasn't yet safe enough to inject into humans. Collip agreed and conducted experiments with rabbits and dogs, while Banting continued other experiments.

He discovered that the process of shrinking the pancreases had been unnecessary. Using whole, fresh pancreases from adult animals worked just as well.

When Dr. McLeod arranged for Dr. Banting to present his results to the American Physiological Society conference at Yale University, Fred was as terrified as he had been as a child in the little schoolhouse in Alliston.

> *"When I was called upon to present our work I became almost paralyzed. I could not remember nor could I think. I had never spoken to an audience of this kind before."*

*The kind doctor was still shy. Unafraid of bullets i*n the front lines of war, a crowd left him speechless. Mcleod, had to come to the podium to help him field questions after the speech, because Banting was tongue-tied.

On the train back to Toronto, Banting sat up all night, beating himself up about his performance. He was humiliated.

"What is wrong with me? Why can't I speak as eloquently as other people? I know the answers. Why is it so hard for me to say them aloud?"

ꙮ

January 22, 1922, was a day for which 14-year-old Leonard Thompson's mother had prayed.

"If you're willing, we'd like to give him a shot of insulin and see how it works," J.B. Collip spoke to Leonard's mother quietly at the sick boy's bedside.

"Yes, please. Whatever you think might help. He's at death's door."

J.B. Collip gave the dying child a shot of insulin. Within days Leonard regained his strength and appetite. Now the team could test this new miracle on other volunteer diabetics. They reacted just as positively as Leonard to the insulin extract. The world needed this new discovery, but how could they make enough for everyone?

"Eli Lily and Company of Indianapolis is willing to work with us to create the serum," Macleod told Banting. "They want you to patent the formula for legal reasons."

"I can't do that." Banting shook his head.

"Why on earth can't you?"

"I've taken the Hippocratic oath. I'm to share freely anything I've learned," Fred explained, looking Macleod in the eye.

"You're dead serious aren't you?" Macleod looked deep into Banting's eyes and admired the integrity he saw there. He shook the good doctor's hand and walked out the door.

Eli Lily and Company of Indianapolis collaborated with Dr. Banting's team to create the formula for insulin, enough for diabetics in North America. Later, Banting was forced to put his name on the patent for legal reasons, but the team gave away all their rights to the University of Toronto.

In the summer of 1922, Toronto received its first batch of insulin, but when the supply faltered in late July, Banting rushed to Indianapolis to see if he could get more. J.K. Lilly wrote:

"We had 150 units ready for him, and when I told him he *could take them back with him, he fell on my shoulder and wept...Banting is really a fine chap.*"

⅋

*Dr. Frederick Grant Banting's fame was painful for th*e shy doctor. Giving speeches terrified him, and he was often tongue-tied when he met new people. His name was in the papers all over the world. The news of his discovery spread outside of Toronto, and in 1923 the Nobel Prize Committee awarded Banting and Macleod the Nobel Prize in Physiology or Medicine.

Every year, the Nobel Prize was given by the Nobel Foundation in Stockholm, Sweden, to people for their achievements in physics, chemistry, physiology or medicine, literature, and for peace. Each prize consisted of a medal, a personal diploma, and a cash award.

The decision of the Nobel Committee to award the prize to Banting and Macleod made Fred angry. The prize should have been presented to him and his assistant, Charles Best. At first, he refused to accept the prize, but after his friends reminded him how greatly it honoured Canada, he changed his mind. However, he insisted on sharing the cash award of $30,000 with Charles Best. Dr. Macleod, in turn, shared his cash award with J.B. Collip.

Diabetes is the leading cause of death by disease in Canada, and insulin was one of the biggest discoveries in medicine. Before Banting's breakthrough, people with severe diabetes suffered terribly and died; others starved to death. Now, as long as people take their insulin, they can live an almost-normal life for a much longer time.

"Insulin is not a cure for diabetes; it is a treatment. It enables the diabetic to burn sufficient carbohydrates, so that proteins and fats may be added to the diet in sufficient quantities to provide energy for the economic burdens of life."

--Sir Frederick Grant Banting, 15, September, 1925

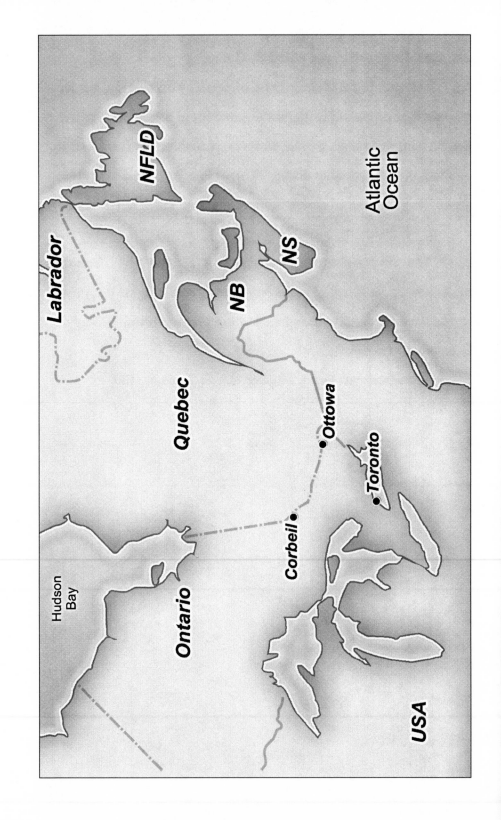

THE DIONNE QUINTUPLETS
BORN MAY 28, 1934

"Multiple births should not be confused with entertainment,

Nor should they be an opportunity to sell products."

–Annette, Cécile and Yvonne Dionne

Marie Reina Alma Dionne
May 28, 1934 - February 27, 1970

I cannot remember entering the world, scrawny, wrinkled, and a miniature of my pint-sized siblings. My mother told me that my four sisters and I were born two months early, on the same day, and in a tired, little farmhouse near the village of Corbeil, Ontario, on May 28, 1934.

I know this is true because our deeply religious Mother never told a lie and also because our birth was announced to the world.

207

When we were only hours old, a newspaperman from *The Nugget* slipped into my parents' house and took a picture of my mother, sisters, and me without asking permission.

"QUINTS BORN TO FARM WIFE."

Words in big black letters splashed across *The Nugget's* front page on the day we were born. Other headlines followed: "25-year-old Corbeil Mother Establishes Canadian Mark…Dr. A. R. Dafoe Says all Five Baby Girls Healthy…" The first words of millions were written about us, and we were never to know the safety of privacy.

Our mother, Elzire Dionne, never wanted anything more in life but to be a good wife and mother. She loved children and was content to have plenty of them. She and our father, Oliva, were devout Roman Catholics who believed that to be blessed with children was to be blessed by God. Before we came along, Mother had already borne seven children: Ernest, Rose Marie, Thérèse, Daniel, and Pauline, who was only eleven months older than us (our brother, Leo, died of pneumonia shortly after his birth in 1930).

The story of our birth, as told to me by my siblings, parents, and the newspapers, was the grandest event in Canadian history during the dark days of the Great Depression. Five babies had never survived being born, and babies rarely survived being two months premature. There were no fancy incubators available to rural Canadians in those days. No one thought we would live more than a few hours, and no one dared hope we would survive the night.

According to the stories I heard and read, our father had been away that day and did not come home until after the early morning hours.

"Get the midwife." Mother groaned and clutched the sheets in pain, as Father dragged his weary body into the house. The house was too small for a private bedroom, so Mother's bed sat in an alcove at the far corner of the kitchen.

Father ran down the road to Aunt Donalda's house and banged on the door at one-twenty in the morning.

"Who is it?" bellowed plump Aunt Donalda, grumpy at being awakened from a sound sleep. She flung the door open.

"It's Elzire. The baby is coming!" Father bounded off the porch and headed toward his truck. "Hurry!"

"But it's too soon!"

Aunt Donalda squeezed into a dress and apron and waddled towards our farm house.

Father drove, as fast as the dilapidated truck would allow, to fetch Madam Benoit Lebel, a midwife who had eighteen children of her own and had delivered hundreds of babies more.

Together the women helped our mother deliver two of us, while Father fetched Doctor Dafoe, who had already delivered six other babies that night. Exhausted, he donned his hat, grabbed his pipe and medicine bag, and followed Father to our house. He found Madam Lebel already tying off two birth-cords with cotton thread from Mother's sewing basket.

"Two babies," beamed Madam Lebel, smiling at Mother.

"I knew there were twins. This pregnancy was so different. But oh, how tiny they are!"

Mother saw how we barely fit in the palm of Madam Lebel's large, able hands.

Dr. Dafoe immediately looked at the two babies and shook his head, exchanging a knowing glance with the midwife. The babies were too small. They would not survive.

"Oh! I need to push again!" Mother cried out in terrible pain.

"Again? Dr. Dafoe--another!" Madam Lebel moved from the bed to allow the doctor room.

"Yes, another."

Dr. Dafoe delivered another tiny babe, and Madam Lebel wrapped it in a clean napkin. Aunt Donalda heated blankets on the stove to cover us and our mother.

"No wonder they are so small," Dr. Dafoe marveled as he looked at us and mother began once again to push another tiny life into the world.

Shortly after the fourth, I was born.

Dr. Dafoe and the midwives glanced at one another and the doctor again shook his head at the midwife. They covered us with the warm blanket from the stove and tucked us into the bottom corner of the giant framed bed. Dr. Dafoe turned his attention to our mother who lay next to us, dying.

Before he left, Dr. Dafoe gave instructions: "Cover Madam Dionne in warm blankets heated on the stove, and baptize the babies.

I'm going to fetch the priest. If by some miracle they live through the night, give them nothing but a few drops of sweetened water from an eyedropper every two hours."

Dr. Dafoe donned his coon skin hat and left our mother and us to die. There was nothing more he could do.

"Ego te baptizo in nomine Patris et Filii et Spiritus Sancti."

One of the women baptized us with a dipper full of water from the bucket in the kitchen. We never knew which one performed the ritual.

During the night, Mother's condition improved slightly, but Father Routhier showed up to anoint her with oil and administer the Extreme Unction. Mother, however, wasn't concerned with dying. She was worried, wondering how she would care for us.

"Five. Five! How will we clothe so many children? Five? What will people say when they find out about this? They will say we are pigs."

She lay in her bed moaning.

Dr. Dafoe wrote in his formal report that night:

"The three larger babies were born first and the two smaller ones last...[they] cry fairly vigorously."

Yvonne Edouilda Marie Dionne
May 28, 1934 - June 23, 2001

I came into the world a miniature human with a lusty cry and a tenacious determination to live. Of course, I don't remember the night of my birth, but I have read so many reports that it seems as if I can.

Following the afternoon of our birth, Madam Lebel borrowed from our neighbor a large wicker basket used for hauling meat. She placed us inside with heated blankets, lit the stove, and set us beside the oven's open door. Later, she took each of us out and gave us a gentle massage with olive oil.

The air was hot and sultry and a thunderstorm brewed, but the stove was kept ablaze as our siblings ran in and out. Pauline, still very much a baby herself, cried for Mother from her crib in the kitchen.

I don't remember how they moved us from the wicker meat basket, warmed with heated bricks, into the laundry basket containing hot water bottles. If any of us looked as though we were fading, Nurse Yvonne Leroux, hired to look after us by Dr. Dafoe, roused and kept us breathing.

We surprised the good doctor by living longer than twenty-four hours.

"We can now feed the babies cow's milk and boiled water. Add two spoons of corn syrup and a little bit of rum," ordered Dr. Dafoe as he inspected each one of us.

"Rum, Doctor?" inquired a surprised Nurse Leroux as she tucked each of us back into the warm basket.

"It will work as a stimulant to keep their hearts beating and them breathing. Brandy would be better, but we can't afford brandy. Feed them every two hours."

Dr. Dafoe turned to my father, who watched from a shadowy

corner of mother's room, "We need breast milk. Mrs. Dionne was never able to nurse her other children, and nursing these babies is out of the question. Mr. Dionne, you must pass the word that your babies need nursing mothers to donate milk."

Embarrassed by such an intimate necessity, our father asked all the neighborhood mothers for help. It wounded his pride to ask for charity, but he did what he must in order to keep us alive.

Together we weighed 13 pounds, 6 ounces. We were the tiniest infants ever to survive. Dr. Dafoe, once a humble, country doctor, became a celebrity overnight. A few days later, Father walked into the house to find the nurses unpacking crates full of breast milk.

"Where did all this come from?"

"The newspapers reported the birth of your babies, and there is breast milk here from Chicago, Toronto, and Montreal," Nurse Leroux beamed as she packed the bottles in ice.

"The United States?"

My father glanced toward us and back at the precious milk.

How many hundreds of women nursed us in those days? We will never know.

A week later, an unfamiliar contraption arrived on our front porch.

"What is this?" quizzed Father as he pointed to a glass box framed with wood, sitting on metal legs.

"It's an incubator for the girls." Dr. Dafoe meandered out to the porch and lit his pipe.

"An incubator?"

Father had never heard of an incubator for babies before.

"See this copper tank here? This we fill with hot water to keep it warm inside. We put a hot wet sponge in that dandy, little holder here on the other side to keep the humidity high. The thermometer you see here on the side will be kept at ninety-degrees Fahrenheit."

"You put my babies in a box? But how will they breathe?"

"There's plenty of air inside, I assure you," sighed Dr. Dafoe as he rolled his eyes and shook his head, "but only three will fit. We'll place the three smallest ones inside."

A few days later another incubator arrived, but it was different. It was heated by earthenware containers filled with hot water which the nurses dubbed "little pigs." As news of our birth spread, donations poured in, including more incubators for each of us. Our parents thought the donations came with no strings attached. They didn't know they were accompanied by the burdensome chains of celebrity.

Outside the farmhouse, crowds gathered, and inside grew the number of willing helpers. By the fifth day after our births, our Uncle Leon Demers stayed to keep the fire in the stove blazing, Aunt Laurence Clusiaux became the family cook and housekeeper, and another nurse was hired to help Nurse Leroux. Dr. Dafoe hired Madam Louise de Kiriline who came in like a hurricane to take charge and bring order and cleanliness to her charges.

"Madam de Kiriline is the Number Two Boss," Dr. Dafoe announced. "What she says, goes as if it came from the Number One

Boss." Dr. Dafoe slapped his chest and left the house.

"First thing that must be done is to disinfect this house."

Madam de Kiriline set everyone to work.

"Mr. Dionne, tack up this netting on the windows to keep out the bugs, and you, Nurse Leroux, get busy scrubbing floors."

In a moment, Nurse Leroux was demoted from the one soul who kept us alive to a mere chamber maid. After the floors and walls were scrubbed, she washed all the clothing, including our tiny diapers. Our 'nappies' flew like white Tibetan prayer flags, 80-strong along the outdoor veranda. Everyone passing by could easily tell something unusual was happening at the Dionne house.

But our diapers weren't the only unusual thing to see in our yard: cameramen and newspaper reporters covered the lawn and spilled out onto the dirt road that ran in front of our house. We were a media sensation. Every paper and newsreel wanted a picture of us, a quote from our parents, and access to our lives.

The nurses lived in tents outside our home, and our brothers and sisters were shuffled off to neighbors and relatives. Our Mother's protests were fully ignored so that we might have every possible chance at life.

"Why must my children be taken away like prisoners?" Mother wept from her bed. She was not allowed to hold us or enter the kitchen area where we were kept. "These are my babies, not their babies! Why must I wear these surgical gowns and masks? A mother knows how to care for her young."

215

"Your other children have bronchitis, and the doctor doesn't want to risk infecting the quints. Please, Madam Dionne, cooperate with us so your girls may live long and happy lives."

Nurse de Kiriline had little sympathy for Mother.

"That nurse thinks she's better than us because she's English," growled Father as he stomped out-of-doors. Thereafter, he avoided the house as much as possible, leaving Mother alone day after day with the strange women telling her what to do in her own home.

The inconceivable miracle of our birth required another miracle for our parents: the money to raise us. Father was a poor dirt-farmer who now had eleven children to feed and clothe. Soon, people offered our father money in exchange for seeing us.

When the newspapers discovered that Father had agreed to exhibit us at a show called "Century of Progress," the story made headlines. But the papers weren't honest. They reported that Father agreed to exhibit us at the World's Fair.

It was a common practice in those days for premature babies to be exhibited in incubators at large fairs. Infant incubators for humans were a new, expensive technology and poor parents of premature infants eagerly agreed to allow their babies to be displayed in exchange for the incubators. When Father made the agreement with the man running the show, he did not believe he was doing anything wrong, because the incubator company would help pay for the expenses of our birth and the supplies we needed.

But Father's actions received harsh criticism, and the

Government of Ottawa placed us in the custody of Dr. Dafoe as special wards of King George V of England by passing "An Act for the Protection of the Dionne Quintuplets." Mother and Father were not educated people, and they did not understand everything that was happening. They did not know whether they had any legal rights, or what to do with them if they had.

Immediately after the act was passed, construction on a brand new house, for my identical siblings and me, began across the road from the farmhouse.

"There will be nine rooms, electricity, central heating, and plumbing," Dr. Dafoe assured my parents. "Every imaginable comfort will be given them."

"I am their mother. I give the comfort my babies need, not a house. My arms, my love," Mother spoke in broken English and jutted her chin toward the doctor.

"Madam, if you want your babies to be healthy, you must trust that we are doing what's best for them," retorted Dr. Dafoe, shaking his head at our mother.

He then leaned over and whispered to Nurse Leroux, "The naïve French."

He did not remember that she, too, was born into a poor, French family.

Émilie Marie Jeanne Dionne
May 28, 1934 - August 6, 1954

The newspapers and newsreels announced that we came into the world pocket-sized and miraculous. I remember not when the new house across the road was built, along with the two-story building for the nurses and policeman. I only know the stories from what I read and heard.

"There are Sacred Heart medals in those walls," Mother whispered to Father as they watched the construction from the upstairs window of the farmhouse.

"How on earth did you…" Father stared at my soft-spoken mother who gazed out the window with fire in her eyes.

"In the middle of the night, I placed them there before the builders closed in the walls. God knows these are my babies, whether anyone else knows it or not. Nothing can change that!" She sobbed, falling into my father's arms. It was becoming a familiar and repeated act, since the day of our births.

To protect us from the world and our parents, Dr. Dafoe ordered builders to erect a seven-foot high steel-mesh fence topped with barbed wire. On a chilly, wet day in late September, our mother's agonizing cries were surely heard in all of Ontario as we were wrenched from her arms and placed beneath the smothering wings of Dr. Dafoe.

The first chapter in our lives in the sterile nursery was photographed and written about more than the lives of any other babies on earth at that time. The single steel-mesh fence wasn't enough to keep visitors at bay, and another had to be erected to keep

218

the thousands of tourists from pouring into our new home.

"The crowds want to see the babies and they are strong enough now to be outdoors. We will take them out on the porch on a rotating schedule."

Dr. Dafoe's wishes were carried out: a nurse held us up one by one, while another nurse flipped a giant name card on the porch's ledge.

"They are too cranky today to be shown," complained our dear Nurse Leroux. "Let me take out Yvette. She's still in a good mood. No one will know. We'll simply change the name card."

Day after day we were paraded up and down the open porch and gawked at like monkeys in a zoo.

"It's not right, Dr. Dafoe. Our babies are not pets. They are people. It's not right to display them this way," complained Father to Dr. Dafoe who always had a ready answer:

"It wouldn't be fair to allow visitors, who drove thousands of miles to see the babies, to go away disappointed."

He puffed on his pipe and pretended that Father was not there.

While Mother and Father mourned in the lonely little farmhouse across the street, we learned to throw kisses, wave, and play pat-a-cake with the nurses in order to please the multitudes. No one noticed the pain in our parents' eyes as they stood abandoned in the yard across the road. They yearned to see us, but they were never allowed.

My first memories—that is, the ones I remember on my own

without having read about them—are of when we began toddling. Madam de Kiriline believed babies should be handled as little as possible. Dr. Dafoe was friendlier and warmer and visited us every day.

"I know of no greater treat in the world than the one I receive when I enter the quintuplets' nursery each morning and see such a rare collection of smiling, healthy babies."

He was extremely proud of us and bragged about "his girls" to anyone who would listen. I think he considered us as his very own.

Every day we climbed onto his lap and he showered us with praise and hugs. It was the warm affection we craved and he was our only constant source of nurturing. We learned to call him 'Papa Dafoe' and he delighted in hearing our sweet, little-girl voices.

"We love you, Papa Dafoe!" we chimed regularly for the cameramen who shared their newsreels with the world.

We had no idea Papa Dafoe exploited us to the press, to companies who used us for advertising, or to the public to raise money for his own purposes. We were too small and trusting. We only knew him as the kind, old man in a shabby, old suit, who smoked a pipe and told us we were pretty.

"Girls, today your mother will come to see you," Dr. Dafoe stood and pulled on his old, coon-skin cap and coat.

"Mother? Who is that?" I was always full of questions.

Dr. Dafoe frowned. How to explain a mother to children who never knew her? The courts said Mother and Father could visit, but

Image: Wikimedia / Ontario Premier Mitchell Hepburn with the Dionne babies 1934

The only life we knew was in our sterile nursery. We had our identical sisters and all the toys, dolls, and pretty clothes a little girl could want. We had our own lovely beds and pint-sized furniture. We had no concept of what lay beyond the walls of our tidy, little home.

All of our desks and chairs were marked by color so we could tell them apart: Annette's things were red, marked with a maple leaf; Cécile had green, with a turkey; Marie's were blue, with a teddy bear; Yvonne's pink, with a bluebird; and my own, white with a tulip.

We did everything together at the same time, every single day. We were on a strict schedule and knew nothing but the routine and the people who surrounded us. We felt safe and secure in our nursery-bubble, blissfully unaware of the war that waged between the adults that surrounded us.

When we reached the age of three, a new observatory was built from which visitors could observe us more closely. A passageway ran along three sides of our playground, and people watched us from behind a window covered with a mesh screen. No one thought we could see them, but they were wrong. We could hear them and see their silhouettes.

"Aw, they're so cute," one shadow spoke.

"Look at her balancing atop the monkey bars," giggled a silhouette with a large feathered hat.

"Someone better catch her before she falls!"

Smoke from a cigar trickled into our play yard and tickled my nose.

"Their matching dresses are so adorable!" The shadowy voices rang out over our little playground day after day as our playful innocence was exploited for dollars.

We purposefully did things to make the shadows laugh. I waded in our baby pool with shoes on and threw my toy monkey into the water. We raced on our tricycles. We learned how to please the crowds because this pleased Papa Dafoe.

Eventually, booths grew up around our home, where souvenirs were sold, and the tourist compound was named "Quintland." There were buildings that sold spoons with our likenesses and names, bumper stickers, post cards, dolls, and more. There were food stands and countless souvenir booths. Many people became quite wealthy on account of us.

But no one could photograph us because *The Nugget* had purchased sole-rights to our pictures. We were considered property instead of babies. One Thanksgiving when we were required to pose with a live turkey, I was the only one brave enough to chase him around the yard with a toy hatchet. My sisters were more frightened of things, but some of those fears were caused by the nurses who cared for us.

One night before being tucked in to sleep, we heard violent scratching on the wall by the door leading to the room in which we all slept together.

"Did you hear that?" asked the nurse as she grinned at us and slanted her eyes.

We all nodded silently.

"What is it?" I piped up.

"Rats. Great, big, giant rats. And if you don't stay in your beds, they will eat you alive. They are bigger than even I. Go to sleep."

The nurses soon learned that to be separated from one another was a punishment difficult for us to endure. A small room at the end of a passageway served as an "Isolation Room." Whenever we were disobedient, we were locked inside this room.

One day, Cécile decided not to obey Madam de Kiriline, who plunked her into the room and locked the door.

"Let me out!"

"No, you will stay in there the rest of the day. Come, girls."

She grabbed my hand and dragged me screaming into the playroom of the nursery, but my sisters and I were inconsolable and stood at the locked nursery door screaming and crying to be reunited with Cécile. Punishing one of us was punishment for us all.

Isolation was not enough for Madam de Kiriline. Sometimes our hands were tied to the head of the bed at night. One evening while tied to our beds, our mother showed up unexpectedly. How did she know something was wrong?

"What is going on? What have you done to my babies?"

Mother immediately untied our wrists.

"This is how you treat my babies? This is how you protect them? What kind of people are you?"

The guards were called, and they threw Mother out of our nursery, but we were never again tied to the beds.

Other nights, we lay in fear of the Sandman.

"RAAUURRR."

We clutched our blankets close to us and trembled as a night nurse walked between our beds warning us:

"If you leave your beds, the monster will get you and take you away. Who knows what he does to little girls? When he takes one, they never come back."

We didn't know the nurse had told one of the guards to growl outside our window.

224

It wasn't nice to influence impressionable little girls this way. My heart was tender and I believed everything I was told. When the nurse read me the story of Old Mother Hubbard's dog, who had nothing to eat, I gave him my bacon the next morning by laying it on the book. The next day, all of us left some bacon for the dog in the book. When the nurse explained to us the dog did not eat bacon but paper, we proceeded each day to bestow him scraps of paper instead.

The dog was not the only one to share our breakfast: Quaker Oats, Libby's, Carnation, and other large food companies began to use our pictures in their advertisements. A movie was made about us. Our guardians signed contracts with the Corn Products Refining Company, Alexander Doll Company, United Drug Company, Tiny Town Togs, Lever Brothers, Palmolive, and others. Everyone benefited financially from us, except for our parents.

Because of our fame, tourists spent $51 million dollars in Ontario in 1934, and two years later they spent almost twice as much. As a result, we brought the government more money through tourism than Niagara Falls.

By the time we were four years old, "Quintland" paid all our living expenses. It also paid the wages and living expenses for the fourteen people working at the nursery.

Our parents never got a dime. They continued to raise our siblings in poverty in the rickety farmhouse across the road. While we dined on the finest foods and wore expensive clothes, our parents struggled to put shoes onto their children's feet and food upon their table.

We didn't know a newspaper claimed us as a $500,000,000 asset to Ontario. We were learning new songs, playing new games, and being little girls. We were unaware of the controversy surrounding us, and we had no knowledge of the greedy people causing our mother and father pain.

Everything we knew and loved was found inside the protective walls where we lived. It was an ideal atmosphere full of pretty, fanciful things made especially for pampered, little girls.

Annette Lillian Marie Dionne
Born May 28, 1934

The first time I saw my other brothers and sisters was through a glass window in the nursery. We had never met them before, and we didn't know who they were. We didn't know what a mother and father were and didn't understand what it was like to have older or younger brothers and sisters.

"Who are they?" Émilie pointed at the spindly children hanging on the gate across the road.

"They are your brothers and sisters," Nurse Leroux whispered so that Madam de Kiriline couldn't hear her.

"What's that mean?" Émilie asked, and we looked at Nurse for answers.

"It means you have the same mother and father."

"Papa Dafoe?" Yvette looked up at Nurse Leroux with wide brown eyes.

226

"Papa Dafoe isn't your father. That man in the hat, standing next to the children, is your father, and the woman holding the baby is your mother."

We eyed the woman with suspicion. The only babies we knew were our dolls. This little person moved and waved his tiny fist in the air. Unknown to us, a year after our birth Mother had given birth to our brother, Victor, but even the birth of a healthy baby boy could not erase the look of sorrow from our mother's eyes.

We never questioned why crowds surrounded our home each day. I suppose we thought all little girls had strangers standing in long lines outside their house. Our knowledge of the world was limited to what we experienced inside the nursery's walls. Nurses dressed in starched, white dresses and stockings took care of us around the clock. Four other little girls who looked exactly like me played, ate, and lived with me in pretty rooms filled with delightful toys.

But our parents never stopped fighting to bring us home. After the death of King George V, Mother wrote a letter to Edward VIII, the new, yet uncrowned king of Great Britain:

"As the date of your coronation is drawing nearer, I simply beg of you to restore to me my five little babies as a 'coronation gift.' Cannot your Majesty understand how I feel without them? Somehow I think you can, for you have an understanding nature, and I know you will extend to me your sympathy and see that my babies are restored to their parents."

In reply, Mother received a form letter acknowledging that her letter was received, but no other answer came.

A short time later, Father began looking for a lawyer who would listen to his story and take him seriously. One of Dad's relatives wrote to *The Nugget*:

> *"If the dog at the Dafoe Hospital can be fed canned milk, cannot a bottle of cod-liver oil be found for the other Dionne children? – One of the Dionnes"*

It wasn't about the money for our Father. By this time he had built, with a partner, his own souvenir pavilion and was more able to support my other siblings from its profits. But Father was a proud man and could not bear the thought of Dr. Dafoe raising his children.

Father wrote to the Pope:

> *"You can understand the natural sentiments of a father, a mother. We want to have our children, and above all we want them to grow up under Catholic influence."*

We were already being brought up Catholic in the nursery, with daily prayers and weekly mass, but, of course, Father did not include that information in his letter. The Pope did not agree to help Father, but he did send him a blessing, which Father framed and hung proudly on his wall.

Six days before our fifth birthday, King George VI and Queen Elizabeth came to visit Toronto. Edward VIII abdicated the throne and, since Mother had written him and received no response, she decided to write a letter to Queen Elizabeth. She asked some friends to help her with English.

When she and father and all our siblings were invited to meet the King and Queen in Toronto, Mother tucked the letter inside her purse:

> *"Is it permitted for a mother who is very unhappy to solicit your kindly intervention to the end that her family be united? You are a mother and, consequently, in a position to realize the sadness that wrings our hearts when we are separated from our five little girls...Let your mother's heart heed my plea and the date of May 22, 1939, will be doubly glorious and unforgettable..."*

To meet the King and Queen, we five walked through the gates of Quintland for the first time since we were four months old. Also, for the first time, the shadows that watched us from behind screened glass came clearly into view, and we made face-to-face contact with strangers.

"Remember, when you see the Queen, be sure to curtsey like this," Madam de Kiriline attempted a curtsey and nearly fell over. She was not amused by our giggles.

"Nurse Leroux, work on their curtseys each day after breakfast and again before bed. Do you understand?"

Nurse Leroux hid her amusement until the older nurse left. She dissolved into laughter with the rest of us, as we practiced how to greet the Queen.

"You must always call the Queen 'Your Majesty.' If she asks you a question, reply, 'Yes, Your Majesty.' Now, pretend that I'm the Queen and walk towards me, one at a time."

Image: Wikimedia / Public Domain / The Dionne Quintuplets arrive in Toronto for presentation to Queen Elizabeth

"Our trip to Toronto will save me a trip to England." Father joked with Mother, who stared out the window and did not speak. It was her first trip on a train too. The two nurses and Dr. Dafoe, who

230

traveled with us, wouldn't allow Mother to interact with us as much as she wanted, and we didn't know her yet as our Mother. She was still a stranger. It bothered our parents that we did not respond to them as little daughters should.

After arriving in Toronto, we changed into our white organdy and old-fashioned poke-bonnets to meet the queen. Each of us wore a different-coloured flower in our hair, so the queen would have no trouble telling us apart: Marie's flower was blue; Yvonne's pink; Émilie's white; Cécile's green; and my own flower was red.

Looking remarkably different in her new, dark blue dress, Mother smiled proudly at each of us and her other children. Father seemed unusually quiet in his dark-gray suit. I thought he looked handsome, but I didn't know him well enough to tell him. Mother's and Father's clothes were nice, but not nearly as fashionable as Dr. Dafoe's, which included a morning coat and tall silk hat. We didn't recognize him without his shabby coat and coon-skin cap.

"The parents and children will meet the King and Queen first. Then, when they are finished, you will be next, Dr. Dafoe."

"But, I thought I would see the King and Queen with the girls, I…"

"Dr. Dafoe, this is a difficult situation; please help us to make it go as smoothly as possible for all those involved."

The royal couple's secretary turned toward our family and ushered us into the presence of the King and Queen.

The drawing room of the Lieutenant General's quarters in the Parliament Building had a soft blue carpet that silenced the tapping footsteps of my new white patent leather shoes. I stared up at the crystal chandelier that twinkled when I squinted. A large mirror hung over the fireplace and reflected the enormous light fixture, making it appear as though two pretty prism-covered lanterns hung in the room. The furniture was designed in the Louis the XVI style, but, I was oblivious. I simply thought it was not as pretty as my little red chair in the nursery.

My feet hurt in my new shoes, and I felt tired and cranky, but when I saw a lady in a powder blue dress smile at Mother and watched Mother curtsy and call her Queen Elizabeth, I tried to remember my manners. Wanting it for myself, I stared at the crown of diamonds upon her head. I decided that when we got home, we would play Queen, so that I could wear one.

The King looked commanding in his admiral's uniform. My hands itched to finger the fringe on the epaulettes on his shoulders and tinker with the jewelled stars and medals that decorated the left side of his chest. There were so many fascinating things for a little girl to see on his dark blue coat: a gold, braided rope hanging down from his right shoulder; a belt around his middle that fastened in front; the glimmering, blue sash and a long sword that looked like great fun. But King George didn't smile and instead looked cross, so I thought better of it.

The Queen's arms were already filled with flowers, but she graciously took each of our bouquets. Marie got confused and handed her flowers to the King, who finally smiled, and Yvonne boldly shook his hand.

Cécile decided to kiss Queen Elizabeth, and we all copied her lead. The Queen stooped down to kiss us all in turn. Papa Dafoe would have never approved, as kisses were not allowed in the nursery. Kisses were couriers of disease.

After the kisses, the Queen presented us with blue, double-breasted coats.

"And this is from my daughters, Princess Elizabeth and Princess Margaret."

The Queen handed a gilded model of a Coronation Coach to Father, and we were enthralled. We could hardly wait to play with it.

Mother spoke shyly with the Queen. Her French accent embarrassed her, but she was also a genuinely bashful soul. And though she wanted her family together more than anything in the world, she simply lacked the courage to slip the queen the letter which she worked so hard and long to prepare.

Cécile Marie Emilda Dionne
Born May 28, 1934

Our happy years in the nursery didn't last much longer after we met the King and Queen of England. Father finally found a good lawyer who could fight to reunite us with our parents. But while the lawyers hashed things out, Father won the right for our siblings to join us in the nursery for school, so we could be educated together. Every day, Daniel, Pauline, and five-year-old Oliva joined us for classes taught only in French. Finally, our parents earned the right to visit us at any time they chose. Every Sunday, we ate the midday meal around the big kitchen table in our parents' house, but, while our parents were happy to have all their children at one table, we were not.

Our parents' house wasn't pretty like the nursery. Our family members were strangers to us. Our other siblings stared at us, whispered about us, and poked fun at us because they were jealous of our clothes and toys. They didn't like us, and we didn't like them. After the meal was over, we could hardly wait to go back to the nursery, which was familiar and felt safe.

When the Ontario Travel Bureau wanted us to do a commercial in English, inviting tourists to Niagara Falls, Father decided to teach us a clever trick: while the program directors drilled us on our lines in English, Father and Mother introduced us to candy, which we weren't allowed to have in the nursery.

"If you do not say anything for the radio man, I will give you more candy," Mother promised.

"Say to the man, 'It's not nice to speak English.'" Father winked and showed us the promised candy. We had no way of knowing that Father spoke English every day of his life. We thought it was absolutely true.

The time came for us to speak on the live radio show.

"So, girls, what do you have to say?" the radio announcer cued us. We were mute.

"Girls, don't you have something to say to the nice people in America?"

We remained silent.

The announcer chuckled uncomfortably, "We seem to be shy today. What do you have to say, girls?"

"It's not nice to speak English!" Yvonne shouted, and we all left our seats and ran to the warm hugs of Mother and Father who slipped us more candy.

Dr. Dafoe didn't speak French, and our father had won a court case demanding that we be taught only in French. After many months of not being able to communicate with us, Dr. Dafoe agreed to give up custody of us and use Quintland funds to build a brand-new house with ten bedrooms, five bathrooms, a playroom, and a music room.

The dining room was big enough for all fourteen of us to sit around the table. It was a pretty house full of gleaming new furniture and delightful rooms.

We liked nice things.

But it was not home sweet home.

And we were not happy.

The first thing Father did when we moved into the house was to place us two to a bedroom. We had never been separated before, and we did not like being apart from one another. Also, we were expected to kiss our parents, whom we barely knew, good night. Love cannot be forced. Nine years had passed since our birth, and we were no longer impressionable, tiny, little girls. We were individuals with our own feelings and autonomy.

Sometimes, I would try to sneak to my room at bedtime

without giving them a kiss, but Mother would fetch me out of bed and force me downstairs to kiss my Father. It made my skin crawl. I wanted to love him the way I had loved Papa Dafoe, but I could not because I did not know him.

"It would have been better if you had never been born," one of our siblings chided.

Another seemed to go out of his way to hurt us.

"Things were better before you came home."

Father insisted we speak French in the nursery, but it was only a ploy against the government which controlled our education. Now that we were reunited with our family, they all spoke English, and all our siblings made fun of the way we spoke. Our English was rusty, and their laughter hurt us.

We turned to one another for comfort, but Father didn't allow it. He wanted us to mingle with the siblings that hurt us. He separated us whenever he could. He never wanted us to think of ourselves as five, but as eleven. The newspaper photos revealed our miserable state of mind. We smiled in very few of our photographs.

A year after we moved in with our parents, Dr. Dafoe died. We cried alone in our rooms and didn't let Father know how sad we were. The fun and happiness we experienced with Dr. Dafoe was something we were never allowed to mention.

Because we were raised in a hospital and had very little immunity to germs, one illness after another befell us in the new house, but the illness that came upon Émilie was terrifying.

236

"You are never, ever, to speak of this," ordered Father, making it extremely clear that Émilie's epilepsy was a shameful thing. In those days, people did not talk openly about seizures. It was only to be whispered in secret. We knew no better.

The first time it happened was during the early morning hours and in the bedroom Émilie shared with Yvonne.

"Come quick! Something's wrong with Émilie!" Yvonne screamed as she banged on our bedroom doors. Instead of going to Mother and Father, she had come to us, her sisters. We too thought we could care for her, but we soon realized we had no choice but to ask for help. After the initial attack, Émilie seized regularly, week after week and sometimes day after day. We learned to slip a spoon into her mouth to keep her from biting her tongue and to sit with her until the attacks passed. Today, there is medicine to help people with epilepsy, but in those days, there was little doctors could do.

We were forbidden to linger in our bedrooms, so we spent as much time as we could together outdoors. In the winter, we went to bed early. But often, Papa would give tours of the house, and we pretended to be asleep when they entered the rooms so we wouldn't be put on display.

Sleep came easily because we were required to do all the chores of the house. We served the field workmen their meals in the kitchen, scrubbed the floors, and cleaned the bathrooms and every inch of plumbing. We milked the cows and fed the chickens. We enjoyed our outdoor chores much more than the inside chores because when we were outside and out of view, we could spend time together.

If an argument began amongst our siblings, we were blamed. For punishment, we had to eat Puffed Wheat for several days in the playroom, while the rest of the family ate steak.

At least when we were alone together in the playroom, we were spared the biting words of our other siblings.

"We were better off before you were born, and we'd be better off without you now!"

"You are a family all by yourselves, and we are the real one."

"Mom wasn't fat before you were born. It's all your fault."

"You split the family in two. You spoiled everything."

Day in and day out, we heard those words, and the guilt weighed heavily on us and caused us to work hard to obey.

Father constantly talked about his concern we would be kidnapped and built a fence around the house to keep strangers away. There were watchdogs and police patrolmen kept on call to escort us. We were never allowed outside the gate without our parents. This kept us from making friends with other children, and we found no friendships with our other siblings. All we had was each other, but we were constantly discouraged from spending time together. All we could do was work. We tossed bales of hay up onto a truck, carried bags of animal feed on our backs, and were careful that no one ever caught us loafing.

We had to pay the price to our family for being born.

We had no idea, until many years after we left home, that the grand house, the food our siblings ate, the clothes they wore, and the cars our parents drove, were all paid for from our work in advertising. Father never told us that money was available. Even after we grew up and moved away, we had no idea how much we were worth.

We didn't know we were million dollar babies.

We thought we were a burden.

If we only knew what we really were – what our mother believed about babies all along. We were a blessing from God.

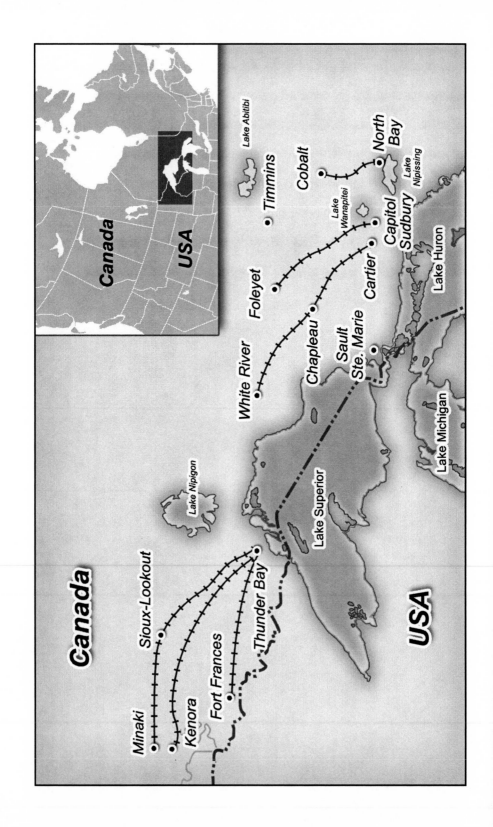

CANADA'S SCHOOL ON WHEELS
1929 – 1967

"We will have to revise our idea of education. Two boys, who could
not write the word 'cat' when they came, wrote social letters after only
seventeen days of schooling."

--Fred Sloman, Teacher, CN School Car #1

January, 1928

"**M**ama! Petunia's in my bed!"

Maggie shivered and hugged the ornery pet skunk close to her face. The snuggly black and white creature's warm softness felt good on her cold nose.

"You kicked your covers off in the night again, didn't you?" Mama chuckled as she moved about the room, folding blankets and straightening pillows.

241

"It's a good thing you made me these warm wool socks for Christmas."

Maggie put toasty feet on the cold linoleum floor. She made her bed with one hand, while holding on to Petunia with the other.

"Put the skunk out, Maggie--that clever little varmint. I don't know how she learned to open the kitchen door."

Maggie heard Mama put wood into the ugly wood stove on the other side of a swinging door that separated the tiny kitchen from the living room.

Her papa, Mr. Sloman, moved about the train car, checking the heating pipes beside the bunks lining the walls.

"I've seen how the little skunk does it. She flops over onto her back and kicks the door until it swings open wide enough for her to flip over and run through."

Mama came through the door and looked at Papa, with both hands on her hips.

"Well, I'll be snickered! Maggie, wake your sisters. The sun will be up and before you know it, the students will have arrived."

"Where are we now? Did we move?"

Maggie looked out the living room window in the train car where she slept with her parents, brother, and three sisters. The frost on the window blocked her view.

Papa moved from the back of the living room at the end of the rail car to the storage area, where the coal was kept, and pulled out a shovel.

242

"Yes, the locomotive hooked up our car late last night, and we're at the Nandair siding now."

"It's a good thing I put the plants in the bathtub," Mama checked her hair in the mirror over the couch and tucked in a few strays. Her braided, golden tresses wound around her head like a halo and sat atop a set of blue eyes that twinkled with energy and good humor.

Mama folded Papa's bed and made it into a small couch.

"Hurry, girls. You don't want Jeremiah Putin catching you in your pajamas."

Billy, Maggie's little brother, barreled past Maggie's bunk and into his mother's skirt.

"Mama, where's Rudy?"

"He's where he's supposed to be, in the box in the classroom. That little fox must be starved by now. You need to hurry and feed him and the other animals."

"Caw!" Jack, hearing his name, cried and flapped his wings. The crow was nearly as smart as the skunk.

"And don't forget to feed Sandy and Cricket." Papa bundled up in a jacket, boots and a hat to shovel the frozen walkway beside the train car steps.

"But it's Margaret's turn to feed the dogs!" Billy pouted and stuck out his bottom lip.

Mama chuckled, "No, remember, you traded Margaret for carrying in wood last night. She said she'd do it if you fed the animals this morning."

"Oh, yeah." Billy ran to care for the family pets.

"Tuck in your shirt, Billy. Girls, hurry up! You still need to do your chores. Elizabeth, raise the Union Jack; Joan, help Fredda get dressed; Maggie, help me with breakfast."

Mama was a skilled, efficient leader and knew exactly what needed to be done and how to assign the jobs.

The Sloman sisters dressed quickly in the cold bedroom, now transformed into a living room by their mother's swift hands. They combed their dark brown hair and dressed in wool, plaid skirts and long, warm socks.

When all the chores were done, everyone gathered at the tiny table where Mama served a hot breakfast of eggs, potatoes, and biscuits she'd made in the enormous oven of the ugly railcar stove. The black range wasn't much to look at, but Mama loved the giant, old stove because "it made the best bread." She poured Mr. Sloman a cup of strong, black coffee, and the children feasted on extra biscuits slathered with creamy butter and Mama's homemade jam, along with a thick slab of back bacon.

After breakfast Elizabeth bundled up to venture out into the frigid cold and hoist the flag at the end of the railroad car. The raised flag signaled to the families of the Canadian wilderness that the little car was open for school.

As Maggie helped Mama clear the dishes, she heard boisterous barking.

"Donna Jean's here!" Maggie shouted when she looked out the

window and saw Donna Jean riding on a sled behind six large, fluffy dogs. Not far behind was Little Arrow in snow shoes, climbing across a snow bank. Beyond the bank came a mother with more children than Maggie could count.

"Papa! I think we have visitors again."

Papa gulped his coffee, pulled on his coat and boots, and ran to greet the mother and her large passel of children.

Mama looked out the window and clucked her tongue, "There's no telling how far they've walked to get here. I better put on more coffee and warm up some biscuits. Who knows if they have had anything to eat."

Mama never allowed anyone to go hungry and played the unofficial roles of mentor and caretaker to the isolated, lonely women of the backwoods. By this time in her husband's teaching career, she had baked a million cookies, delivered dozens of babies, and taught hundreds of women to read, sew and care for children. She busied herself in the primitive kitchen and stoked her woodstove to heat the oven, while Maggie helped her little sisters finish dressing themselves and organizing their homework.

Students arrived at the back of the schoolroom section of the little train car, politely removed their boots and scuttled into the narrow room in stocking feet. The new woman's children had never seen a school or a desk before. They sat backwards on top of the desks with their feet on the attached chair. Billy showed one of the boys the proper way to sit in the desk, and they all followed his example. They were quiet and polite, whispering to one another in Italian as none of them spoke English. Elizabeth counted heads: twenty-two.

Mr. Sloman motioned to Maggie.

"Take Mrs. Lombardi and the babies to see Mama, while I get the children settled and enrolled in school."

Maggie took two toddlers by the hands and showed the pale, exhausted woman holding a tiny baby, to Mama's kitchen. The bedraggled mother tripped over two runny-nosed preschoolers hanging onto her tattered coat.

Mama held up the coffee kettle and offered, "Coffee?"

The dark-eyed woman nodded quickly and Maggie pointed to a chair. The weary mother focused with hungry eyes on Mama as she poured a steaming cup of coffee. Maggie motioned to the sleeping baby and the woman handed her to Maggie.

"School? My kids?" the woman asked in halting English. Maggie recognized the Italian accent right away. Another student attending school in the train car was also from Italy.

"Yes." Mama offered the shivering mother a hot biscuit and honey.

"No railroadman husband--lumberman." The woman frowned and shook her head. Her dark eyebrows slanted together above a sturdy, upturned nose.

"Oh, this school isn't only for railroad children. It's for all children of Canada," reassured Mama as she motioned her arms in a big circle, as if she was embracing all the children of the great commonwealth.

246

"Si? All?"

Mama nodded, "Yes, all–everybody."

Mama was well-educated and understood Italian, but she always used English to help the new families assimilate. Maggie admired her mother's warm hospitality. She looked lovely, framed in the sunbeam of light streaming in from the narrow cabin window, where they sat at the tiny kitchen table.

The woman's face lit up with a crooked smile that revealed two missing teeth behind a set of chapped, curved lips. A tear slid down her cheek.

Mama patted her hand, "You can stay today and watch. If you want, you can come back on Thursday for the mother's meeting, and I can help you learn to read English, too." Mama spoke as if the woman understood, but pulled a notebook out of a drawer and drew pictures of a calendar, illustrating what she was trying to explain.

The baby in Maggie's arms seemed terribly still. Maggie felt her tiny forehead. She was burning up!

"Mama, this baby is sick!"

∞

Elizabeth helped her father settle his pupils into their seats. Fortunately, some of the new family's children were small, and they were able to sit two to a seat. The little classroom only held twelve desks: six along each wall of the railroad car. Mr. Sloman put a small chair beside each desk to accommodate as many students as he could.

Joan turned to her father and held her nose. He smiled back at her. The smell of garlic, wet boots and goose grease rubbed on the children's chests to protect against illness, grew stronger as little bodies warmed up. There was no running water for baths in the Canadian outback, and some children never changed their clothes or their underwear the entire winter, which only added to the startling aroma.

Finally, every child was enrolled and had a pencil and some paper. Elizabeth watched out the window as the dog team that brought Donna Jean to school ran towards her father's hunting cabin, where she lived with her mother. Without being prompted, they would return for her on their own at four o'clock.

"Okay, children, write whatever you wish," encouraged Fred Sloman, who had to learn what each child knew. "You may draw a picture, if you like."

Without prompting, English-speaking children helped the new students understand what the teacher meant. Before long, Mr. Sloman knew with a glance at what learning level each student belonged. For the first part of the day, most of his students would start with the alphabet, several would gather around a science text, and a smaller group would continue their study of geography. Only four of his students' primary language, aside from his own children's, was English.

Elizabeth's group studied the geography of the Mediterranean, and Mr. Sloman saw one of the older Lombardi twins' eyes light up at the sight of the little boot-shape on the map tacked to the wall.

"Italia! La mia casa!" The boy waved at Mr. Sloman and pointed his pencil in the air towards the map.

"*Si*. Italy *was* your home, but now your home is Canada." Fred Sloman picked up the globe and showed the fifteen-year-old boy where he lived in Canada, then slid his finger towards Italy.

"I am Mr. Sloman. What is your *nome*—name?"

"Il mio nome è Antonio."

"Pleased to meet you, Antonio." Mr. Sloman pointed to Elizabeth. "Her name is Elizabeth."

"Name," sounded Antonio as he drew out the sound of the 'a.' "Name, Antonio."

"Name?" Elizabeth pointed to each of his siblings.

"Maria, Zita, Mimi, Belinda, Dino, Bianca, Viviana, Guido, Vittoria, Carla, Sienna, Dante, Pino, Orlando, Enrico, Giacamo, Luigi, Santo, Sergio, Vincentio, e bambino e Gina." rattled Antonio so quickly, Elizabeth couldn't catch them all. But Mr. Sloman's keen ears caught each one, and he wrote them on his class diagram. He quickly went to each child, called them by name, and introduced himself.

The two family dogs made themselves known, tails wagging as they sniffed the goose lard rubbed on each child's chest. The children read or talked to the dogs, and showed them the pictures in books. Elizabeth finished her geography lesson, and Joan helped her father teach the little ones the alphabet, using the name of an animal for each letter.

Out of nowhere five-year-old Carla wailed soulfully in Italian. Some of her siblings giggled uncomfortably while the older sister, Bianca, comforted her little sister.

"What's wrong?" begged Fredda, filled with concern. .

Mr. Sloman was familiar with several languages, but the language of a hungry child was not that difficult to understand.

"She's starving. Go tell Mama we need biscuits."

Before Elizabeth could open the kitchen door, Maggie entered the little classroom carrying a tray of biscuits and small glasses of fresh milk. The children ate them so ravenously, the Sloman girls were afraid they would choke.

"No one can learn on an empty stomach. After they eat, we'll go outside for a spell." Papa took a swig of coffee and reached for his hat and coat.

"But Papa, it's 42-degrees-below outside," cried Maggie as she pointed to the thermometer at the window.

"It's okay. Tell your Mama we'll take the little ones, too, if she wishes."

Maggie shook her head, "I don't think that'd be a good idea. The baby is awfully sick. Mama will probably want the other little ones to stay indoors."

"What's wrong with the baby?"

"Mama thinks it's the croup. She's fixing a poultice and showing Mrs. Lombardi how to make it herself. I've been keeping the baby cool with a washcloth. She has a terrible fever, Papa. I'm awfully worried."

Mr. Sloman checked the baby and headed outdoors to be with the other children.

"I believe in plenty *airing out* time. It makes for the best learning."

After a quick recess, the children returned inside and Mama met them with steaming cups of hot cocoa and gingersnaps. While the children snacked, Mr. Sloman read aloud from *Alice in Wonderland*. He acted out the story with such expression that the students could easily comprehend the story, even with a limited understanding of English.

After more studies it was time for lunch, but Mrs. Lombardi hadn't brought any food. Mama quickly made butter and egg sandwiches, and every child had another biscuit with honey. With every tummy full, every mind was primed for learning. When it was finally time to go home, no one wanted to leave.

The baby's temperature had significantly reduced, and Mama helped Mrs. Lombardi bundle up her brood and walk them home. She packed a basket of food and home-supplies to take with her.

"I'm going to go see what else she needs. Later, I'll send a message with the passing train and get more supplies here before we move on. Joan, you and Maggie get dinner ready and don't wait for me. Go ahead and eat when it's ready."

Mama walked five miles in the bitter cold to the shanty where Mrs. Lombardi lived with her husband and their twenty-two children.

It seemed remarkably smaller than the school train. Along the inside walls of the rickety structure and upon a rough-hewn floor lay piles of blankets used for beds. There was not a stove, only a fireplace and hearth for cooking food in a large pot. The only food in the house was a can of beans sitting on the homemade table. The linens – what there were of them – were clean. No closets or armoires could be seen. Mama assumed that the only clothes the family owned were those they wore.

"How does she live?" Mama talked to herself as she trudged the five miles back to the railroad car in the deep snow and bitter cold. She never felt afraid. Her body was strong from years in the Canadian wilderness, washing clothes by hand and walking for miles to visit her husband's students and their families. And tonight, as she walked in the light of a quarter-full moon, she had a companion. A lonely dog nuzzled next to her, searching for her hand.

"Hello there, old boy, what are you doing out here by yourself in the cold?" Mama patted the canine on the head and continued to trudge through the snow toward the coal lights, beaming from the welcoming windows of the train car. She hoped Maggie and Joan remembered to make supper.

When she finally reached home, Mr. Sloman greeted her with a sweater warmed by the blazing stove in the kitchen.

"Brrr, it's a cold one–thank-you." She removed her coat and wrapped the warm sweater around her shoulders, hugging herself. "That poor dog outside walked me home and kept a close eye on me all the way. He has to be hungry and freezing. Let's get him something to eat."

Mr. Sloman peeked out the window and peered down at the dog pacing back and forth beside the train car.

"Mama, that's not a dog."

Mama looked down at the poor beast running beneath the window.

"What do you mean? He's right there."

"Mama, that's no dog; that's a wolf."

"Well, if I had known he was a wolf I wouldn't have patted him on the head!"

❧

The next day all the children returned. With the children, Mrs. Lombardi sent lunches made from the supply of staples Mama had taken to her shanty the night before. This time, only eighteen of the children came.

Antonio smiled at Mr. Sloman.

"Baby-okay."

"That's good news, very good news!" Mr. Sloman returned the boy's smile and motioned for him to take a seat.

Danny rushed in from the back of the school car.

"Help! Molly's stuck in a snow bank and can't get out!"

Mr. Sloman grabbed his coat and ran to the snow bank where little Molly lay with her skis sticking straight up out of the snow. With the help of two of the boys, Mr. Sloman pulled Molly out of the bank. Her bright red face shimmered with frozen tears.

"You're okay, Molly. We've got you." Mr. Sloman brushed the snow off the little girl's rabbit-fur coat.

"I know I'm okay. I'm not hurt. I'm mad!" Molly hiccupped with willful sobs.

"Why are you angry?" Mr. Sloman bent down to Molly's level.

"Because I wanted to be the first one to school today."

As always, the school day brimmed with individual studies for each child. Everyone recited multiplication tables and labelled the towns on a map of Ontario. They painted a watercolour of their favourite forest animal and made a spelling list from words they could use when writing a letter. Because the school car only came to each site one week each month, Mr. Sloman assigned each child a poem to memorize and recite upon his return.

When it was time to go home, the children did not want to leave. They were fascinated with practising their new skills. Most of them had learned to write their names, and the older boys could sound out a few words in English and solve two-digit sums. Mr. Sloman sent home enough homework to keep each child busy for more than an hour each night. He also sent with them paper, pencils and books.

"I leave on Friday. That means we only have four days of school here before we break for one month. On Thursday I will leave you with homework to do each day while I'm gone. Understood?"

Mr. Sloman's passion was reaching out to the isolated children of Canada and making the most of his time with them.

The children were eager to learn and at the end of the day when it was time to say good-bye, a few cried.

"Don't worry. We'll be here tomorrow," Billy reassured them and the Sloman girls hugged them all good-bye.

It took a lot of work getting supper ready each evening and helping their own children with their homework each night, but Papa and Mama were not afraid of hard work. They laboured together like a well-oiled set of gears: Mama kept the stove warm and Mr. Sloman kept the water pipes from freezing; Mama cooked and Papa helped with dishes.

Finally, after the younger children were asleep, Maggie and her parents enjoyed a hot cup of coffee in the schoolroom before going to bed.

"Another cup, Papa?" Maggie picked up her father's empty cup.

"Yes, Maggie, thank-you."

"Mama?"

"If you please. Just bring the pot out here."

Mama smiled but her eyes looked tired.

Maggie went into the kitchen to get the coffee pot, but as she reached for the pot she heard something move inside the stove. She opened the oven door and screamed, "Papa! There's a man in the oven!"

CB

"He's probably cold."

Papa and Mama pulled the man out of the oven and sat him at their kitchen table. He had broken into the train car and crawled inside the oven to get warm. Mama heated up a pan of soup, and Maggie made another pot of coffee. The man's hands shook so badly that Mama had to hold the cup to his mouth. He drank cup after cup of coffee and soup.

"It's 60-degrees-below out there tonight." Papa pointed to the thermometer by the window.

The man didn't speak English, but words weren't needed. Someone was cold, hungry, and in need of shelter and food. The school-car shined the only light around for miles in the wilderness. And though the Slomans were warned by the Canadian National Railroad to pull their blinds at night to reduce the risk of break-ins, Mr. Sloman refused.

"Let there be light! Mrs. Pasquale told me she sat up all night to watch our lights. Ever since then, I don't have the heart to pull the blinds. We're the only light in this bleak wilderness some folks ever see."

The two gasoline lamps in the school car ceiling sent out much brighter light than the coal oil lamps along the side of the car.

"More than one lonely woman sits up at night with a sick child and watches our lights," Mama agreed with Papa. The lights would stay on and the blinds would stay up.

256

Mr. Sloman helped the cold man settle in to sleep on the floor with some of Mama's warm quilts. They felt no fear of him and their kindness was repaid in the morning with a simple thank-you as the man again ventured out into the snow.

"I wonder how he'll survive out there." Mama shook her head. But she didn't have time to worry about the lone man as children arrived for school. Today would be a long day. She had plenty to do to get ready for the evening, when Mr. Sloman would teach the men of Nandair how to write their names and speak English. There were cookies to bake and warm soup to get started, along with bread for her family.

"Mama, look at Fredda's dress. There's soot all over it!" Joan pushed little Fredda towards Mama.

Fredda pointed to the smudge on her dress.

"Soot! Soot, Mama!"

Mama sighed. She'd grown used to the smell of grease, coal and steam, but the constant soot from the railroad was still a bone of contention with her.

"It'll have to do. Wipe it off as best as you can for now, Joan. Thank-you."

"Yes, Mama." Joan ushered little Fredda to the kitchen sink and cleaned the dress.

Mama never wasted time complaining and her hands were always moving. As much as she would like to wash the railroad soot off her curtains, deep cleaning would have to wait until spring. It was too cold to wash them now. Her city friends wouldn't abide by the hardships she endured, but compared with what the lonely families of the wilderness lived, she recognized hers as a life of luxury.

The school-car's small classroom sheltered children from different countries at different levels of learning. The bigger boys seemed embarrassed that they could not write as well as the younger children, but Mr. Sloman put them at ease right away. He balanced phonics, writing and arithmetic with hands-on projects. The wilderness children may not have been good at academics at first, but they all excelled at using their hands.

Image: Wikimedia / Public Domain / Photo of inside of school-car taken by Wintershom

"Let's draw a train today and count the cars," Mr. Sloman pulled out a roll of adding-machine tape and laid it out the length of the car. The children went straight to work drawing their own train.

"Where do you think the trains go?" Mr. Sloman walked behind the children, watching each one as they worked, picking up on their strengths, and recognizing their weaknesses.

"Italia!" cried a grinning Dino.

"Ireland!" answered Molly as she raised her hand.

"Toronto!" guessed Gerald, who had never been there though he had heard of it.

"One of you is correct. Trains do go to Toronto, but they don't go all the way from Canada to Italy or Ireland. Who can tell me why?"

"They run out of coal?" Billy stuck out his tongue in concentration as he decorated his train car.

"Clever answer. They could indeed run out of coal, but that's not why."

"Trains can't swim!" yelled Donna Jean, not looking up from her drawing of a purple freight car.

"Very good, Donna Jean. They can't! Why does this matter?"

"Because they must cross the big water." Little Arrow walked to the map and pointed to the Atlantic Ocean.

"Excellent, Little Arrow! Between Canada and Italy and Ireland, there is a large body of water called the Atlantic Ocean. So, how do you think people travel there instead?"

"A big canoe!" Little Arrow held up his finger in revelation.

Donna Jean giggled, "Big ship. I had to go on one when my Papa brought us here."

"That's right! A passenger ship that…"

A steam locomotive pulling a long line of freight cars flew past the little school-car parked on the side of the tracks, drowning out Mr. Sloman's lecture. The windows rattled and the books danced on the shelves. The children ran to the window to watch it fly by. Mr. Sloman shook his head and put his hands in his pockets. Many teachable moments were interrupted by the blasting of a freight train on its way to somewhere else.

That evening, railroadmen, lumbermen, and others gathered at the little school to learn how to write their names and to speak English.

"They hold their pens so tight the blood runs out of their hands," Mama said.

While Mr. Sloman taught the men, the women gathered with Mama in her cramped living-quarters to learn sewing and dressmaking. She also taught them hygiene, Canadian history and how to speak and write in English.

The Sloman family spent one week with the children and families who lived along the Nandair stop, before moving on to the next stop for their school on wheels.

On Thursday nights, Mr. Sloman turned down the gas lights and checked the pipes before going to bed.

"The hard part, Mama, is wondering if I'll ever get to see those children again."

☲

The Slomans never knew when the locomotive would hook up to their little school-car and take them to the next wilderness area, parking them on a siding where they would stay for five or six days until they moved again to the next location. Once school let out on Thursday, the family secured all their belongings in case they were hooked up in the middle of the night. Sometimes the dishes broke anyway because the locomotive slammed into the coupling with a jolt.

Maggie took down the flagpole hanging on the end of the school car, then they gathered in all the outdoor toys: toboggans, skis, and sleds. They took down the clothesline and packed all of Mama's pretty tea-servings.

Papa put anchors on the gas lamps so they wouldn't fall off the hooks on the ceiling. The girls cleared the countertops of dishes, and all the cupboard and refrigerator doors were firmly shut. Mama filled the portable bathtub with her treasured plants. The locomotive could come during the next day or during the night while they slept, but it always came and took the little car and the teacher's family to the next wilderness site where children eagerly awaited its arrival.

During the weekend, Papa planned lessons, and Mama organized and cleaned their tiny home. On Monday, Papa asked Margaret to raise the flag on the school-car, signifying a cheerful welcome to the students in the area of Foleyet.

Earlier that morning, more than ten miles away, the Dingee children, ages nine, eleven and twelve, began their journey to school on their eight-foot toboggan, pulled by five energetic, barking dogs.

"Don't forget to pick up Kitchi and Moki!" Betty reminded her older brother, Francois. They liked to meet up with their native friends along the way to school.

"I won't! You don't need to remind me. They'll be waiting on the trail."

The dogs ran eagerly and needed little reminding of the route.

Betty snuggled into her warm fox-coat and hid her nose in the fur. Her father was a trapper, and she was thankful for the warm furs he brought home. She hugged herself and wiggled her frozen toes inside the buckskin moccasins her mother had made. Nothing would stop her from going to school. Not even frigid temperatures or snow and ice.

They arrived at the banks of the frozen lake where they met Kitchi and Moki. Nearby stood an old trapper's cabin. The wind and snow blew through the slats in the log walls, but it would be home for the children for the week they were at school. The girls helped Francois unpack the food and blankets. They repacked the bag with their books and homework and headed out and into the cold for another two-mile trek.

"Help me to tie the dogs, Alice."

The girls and native boys tied up the dogs while their big brother repositioned the pack upon his back. Everyone attached their snow shoes and set out across the frozen lake. Every thirty feet, they marked the trail with an evergreen branch in case the wind covered their tracks.

When Mr. Sloman saw the children approach, he bounded out the door to greet them. He was impressed with their commitment and that night shared his awe with Mama, "I'm amazed how far they travel to school. They're starving for knowledge!"

Nine-year-old George and twelve-year-old Nicholas travelled forty-two miles to get to school. They worked beside the school-car, pitching a canvas tent against a snow bank. They found an old wood stove and installed it with the pipe sticking out of the canvas roof. Before going inside to warm themselves, Kitchi and Moki helped George and Nicolas thatch the fragile tent with evergreen boughs. This fortified tent would be home to George and Nicholas for a week in frigid weather. It was too far to travel back and forth for each visit.

On Mondays, children trickled into school during the morning because travel for some was hard. Not everyone arrived on time, but, remarkably, no one arrived more than a few minutes late. Mr. Sloman had given them enough homework for a month, and they eagerly shared their hard work with him.

Finally, everyone settled into a gentle hum of industry. Younger students rehearsed phonics, and the older children who needed the practice, joined in. Mr. Sloman's daughters learned Shakespeare, while others their age studied sentence structure. Everyone learned at different rates and every child received individual attention by their astute teacher. He customized the lessons, loaned out books, and created learning plans for each student, including his own children.

While one group recited multiplication tables, another looked up words in the dictionary. While some studied medieval history, others labeled towns on the map, and still others chanted rules of grammar. They all memorized poetry. There was never an empty moment. Everyone learned.

On Tuesday, while everyone listened to a chapter in *Alice in Wonderland*, a woman stumbled into the school car.

"Help me."

"Mama!" cried Davey Pacelli as he ran to his mother who collapsed on the floor.

"Maggie, go get your mother. Joan, help me get Mrs. Pacelli to the living room." Mr. Sloman's gruff voice and stern face sprung Maggie into action.

Joan and Mr. Sloman helped Mrs.Pacelli into the little cookery, but she was too weak to make it to the living room and collapsed in their arms.

"My…baby…"

"Put her down here, Joan."

They helped the frail mother-to-be to the floor, while Mama rushed to their aid.

"Mr. Sloman, leave the girls here with me. I will help her. Keep the children calm. Joan, boil a big pot of water and, Maggie, you know the old sheets I keep under the bed? Bring me two of them. I'm also going to need a thick blanket. And find every clean towel you can and bring it here."

264

"Yes, Mama," chimed both girls as they set to work, immediately obeying their mother.

"My…I'm so tired…" Mrs. Pacelli whispered.

Mama felt her pulse.

"When was the last time you ate something?"

"Yesterday."

Maggie brought the blanket and sheets and helped her mother tuck them under Mrs. Pacelli, who was too weak to move. The woman moaned and held onto her stomach.

"Where is your husband, Mrs. Pacelli?" Mama asked loudly.

The ashen woman writhing on the floor did not answer.

"Mrs. Pacelli, where is Mr. Pacelli?" begged Mama as she knelt beside the woman and spoke into her face, framing it with her hands.

"He's out hunting. I haven't seen him…in days…I…Ohhh!" Mrs. Pacelli rolled on to her side and clutched her stomach, crying out in pain.

"Joan, tell your father to take the children outside or begin an activity to distract them."

"Yes, Mama."

"Mrs. Pacelli, try not to cry out. I know it's hard, but we don't want to frighten the children." Mama made a knot in a towel and gave it to the woman. "Bite on this when you want to scream. It might help; it might not."

The woman could not hold onto the cloth. Mr. Sloman entered the room and stood over his wife and the sick woman.

"Do you need me in here, Mama?"

Mama nodded, "I think so. Do you think it would be okay for Maggie and Joan to take the children outside and for you to help me in here instead?"

Mr. Sloman nodded and turned to the girls, "Joan, Maggie, tell the children school is dismissed for the day. Then, take your siblings outdoors until I tell you to come back inside."

The girls nodded and scooted out the kitchen door. Mr. Sloman rolled up his sleeves and set to work boiling water and helping his wife.

"Ohhhh! It's not time! It's too early…" groaned Mrs. Pacelli, whose face contorted with pain.

"Babies don't read calendars. They have their own ideas of when it's time to come." Mr. Sloman handed Mama a cold cloth for Mrs. Pacelli's head and turned to add wood to the stove.

With the kind help of Mr. Sloman and Mama, a tiny baby boy was born on the kitchen floor of the school-car. Tiny and weak, he could hardly breathe. Mama wrapped the baby gently in a clean towel and handed him to his mother, who lay on the floor sobbing. She looked at Mr. Slocum with tears in her eyes. The baby was not well.

"Will you baptize him, Mr. Sloman?"

Mr. Sloman gathered the sick baby in his arms. "He's a handsome little man."

"What is his name?" asked Mama, brushing a tear from her cheek.

Mrs. Pacelli looked into Mama's eyes and whispered, "Emmanuele Alberto."

Mr. Sloman nodded and christened the tiny baby according to his mother's wishes. Shortly after the christening, little Emmanuele drew his last breath.

In one short day a tiny soul tasted life on both sides of heaven.

ಜ

December, 1928

Sandy and Cricket barked in encouragement as Mr. Sloman and Billy dragged a little cedar tree through the snow towards the school-car. This was Billy's favourite time of the year. Most boys and girls celebrated Christmas once each year, but the Sloman family celebrated it for the entire month of December. As the school-car stopped in each wilderness area, their family celebrated the holiday with each community.

There were no churches in those remote areas. There were no stores or nativity scenes. The only kind of Christmas the children in the Canadian wilderness enjoyed was what the Sloman family provided.

All through the year, the Imperial Order of the Daughters of the Empire collected clothing, toys, and household utensils as gifts and prizes for the school children of the remote areas of Canada. Each Christmas, every family received a gift box.

On the chalkboard Joan wrote "Merry Christmas" in

all the languages of the school children: *Buone Feste Natalizie* (Italian); *Srozhdestvom Kristovym* (Ukrainian); *Wesolych Swiat Bozego Narodzenia* (Polish); *Feliz Navidad* (Spanish); *Gledelig Jul* (Norwegian); *Fröhliche Weihnachten* (German).

Families from these nations came to the wilderness to log, mine, trap, and maintain sections of the railroad. The only Native language Mr. Sloman knew how to write was Iroquois. Joan wrote in small letters across the top of the chalk board: *Ojenyunyat Sungwiyadeson honungradon nagwutut.*

Billy and the girls helped Mr. Sloman pull the tree into the school-room, while Mama baked cookies and cinnamon rolls in the oven. Elizabeth stood on a desk and held the tree upright, while Mr. Sloman fastened a laundry line to the tip and secured it to the top of the window sill.

"Sandy, stop eating the popcorn!"

The golden retriever looked up at Joan with a string of popcorn hanging out of his mouth.

"He's going to choke, Papa! Get him!"

Maggie laughed and helped her father pin the playful dog, who rolled over onto his back asking for a belly rub and willingly giving up his prize. But as soon as they secured the popcorn, Cricket jumped on a desk and nosed into the tree.

"He thinks something is in there."

Billy put his head in the tree right beside Cricket's.

"There probably is. Animals live in trees. Can you name some?"

Mr. Sloman never ceased teaching.

"Birds live in trees," peeped Little Fredda from the floor where she sat making a gingerbread paper-chain.

"Yes they do. Can you think of anything else?"

Papa hung ornaments on the trees.

"Koalas live in trees," Billy giggled from inside the tree.

"They do, don't they, Billy. Why is that funny?"

"There aren't koalas in Canada, Papa." Billy backed out of the tree. "I don't see anything."

"You didn't, but Cricket did." Maggie pointed to the big shaggy dog holding a bird's nest in his mouth.

Mr. Sloman rescued the frail nest from the dog's jaws.

"Can you tell what kind of bird lived in this nest?"

The children peered at the nest cradled in their father's hands, a tiny grass and pine needle cup, lined with feathers like the ones on Mama's favourite hat. A rubber band, a piece of yarn and birch bark were also part of the little bird's home design.

"Well, it's quite small, and by the way it's shaped, I think it's probably a tree swallow, Papa."

Joan loved nature studies.

Mr. Sloman beamed, "You're right! This is a little tree swallow nest. Let's add it to our collection."

He put the nest on a shelf along with all the other treasures from nature studies of the past.

"Cricket's got a good nose, Papa!" Fredda patted the dog's head.

"Dogs have more olfactory receptors in their noses," shared Mr. Sloman, stepping back to admire the tree.

Mama stood in the door of the kitchen, holding it open with her foot.

"Well done, children. The tree looks very festive." Mama wiped her hands on her apron.

"Are the cookies done yet?" asked a hopeful Mr. Sloman, who loved Mama's cookies, especially with a hot cup of coffee.

Mama laughed, "I didn't think you'd last long. After we finish decorating the rest of the car, we'll enjoy cookies and warm milk. How does that sound?"

Everyone cheered and finished decorating the railcar with evergreen boughs and the popcorn and cranberries they had strung days before. It smelled altogether like Christmas.

"I don't know how we'll keep Cricket and Sandy from eating the popcorn," Joan groaned.

"What about Jack?" Bobby pointed to the crow preening outside the door of his cage.

Mama laughed, "He'll probably eat it too. Joan, when you were a little sprout, I'd find you hiding behind the tree, eating popcorn hand over fist."

Everyone laughed and Joan blushed.

"Can I help it if I have more taste buds than you?"

"And how do you know that?" Mama grinned.

"Because, when one's young, one has more taste buds than

when one's older," Joan giggled. Like her father, she enjoyed surprising her family with random facts.

"I assure you, my taste buds are all in working order," teased Papa as he patted his flat tummy. He took pride in being fit, but liked to pretend that he looked fat. "Your mother's cooking is not to be missed. Now, let's get to those cookies!"

During the entire month of December, the little train-car, with its cheery Christmas decorations and Mama's cookies, travelled from site to site, spreading Christmas joy and cheer with each stop. Every class put on its own Christmas pageant and held its own parties. The children made paper chains and stars with glitter, and the time spent at each site culminated with a Christmas pageant, complete with live animals for the nativity.

At the Kakatush site, the families went an extra mile for their Christmas party: all the children wore homemade costumes. Gerald Buck dressed as a shepherd and brought a baby lamb with him, for an authentic Christmas scene in the stable. Little did anyone know how much the little lamb enjoyed Christmas carols.

All the inhabitants of the train-car sat in silent awe as the climax of the nativity ended with Sarah Brown, with a voice as clear as Mama's crystal, singing "O Holy Night." No one dared stir as she sang with a voice so pure. It brought tears to reverent eyes.

"Faaaaall on your kneeees…O heeeeear the angel voiiiiices… Oh niiiiiiight diviiiiine…"

"BAAAAAAAA." The little lamb joined in the chorus.

The intense, sacred moment shattered as the inhabitants of the train-car stifled giggles.

With every strain, little Sarah sang louder.

And with every note, the little lamb turned up the volume of its bleating.

Before the end of the song, the entire train-car filled with laughter. Sarah finished the song, holding the musical lamb in her arms.

"Perhaps this also happened on the first Christmas," Mr. Sloman laughed.

After the program, Mr. Sloman took his gramophone to the river, and while some skated to the music, others picked teams and played a quick game of hockey.

At the end of each party, the Slomans gave gifts of clothing, food, and household items. In exchange, they received chickens, rabbits, home-baked goods, and fresh cream. During the gift exchange, Pasquale Deciccio walked down the aisle and planted a bottle of whisky on the teacher's desk.

"Why on earth did he do that?" Mama clucked after the party.

"Perhaps in his land it's a custom." smiled Papa as he scratched his head.

When Christmas Eve arrived, the Sloman family had spent an exhausting month celebrating Christmas, and that was the night when the pipes in the school-car froze and their cozy home had to be towed back to Caperol, to the roundhouse, to thaw out. The family spent

Christmas day singing carols with the men of the roundhouse and celebrating Christ's birth with strangers.

Much the same as Mary and Joseph did the day baby Jesus was born.

Spring 1929

"Bring more water from the river, Maggie. Joan, bring me that other basket of clothes, then boil the water Maggie brings and check the bread in the oven."

"Yes, Mama."

Mama's oldest girls were an invaluable blessing. Life on the railroad-car was often hard. The chores never ended, but Mrs. Sloman kept a tidy car and neat children and never complained. Her cooking was unmatched by other women in the wilderness. By her example, women learned how to be good housewives and mothers.

Mama wiped her brow and looked at the murky water in the washtub.

"Getting this soot out of the curtains is an impossible job. The water turns black as soon as I put them in the tub, and it takes a lot of water to rinse it out."

The only running water on the train was cold water. Washing the soot out of curtains took hot water boiled on the stove. But Mrs. Sloman was thankful for spring time. She wanted to finish the washing so she could plant red geraniums, paperwhites, and begonias in the boxes on the school-car window ledges.

Inside, Mr. Sloman bent over a spreadsheet organizing a Coinuckle tournament for the monthly community game-night. Bingo was another favorite and, while it bored Mr. Sloman, the game allowed all ages and languages to play.

"Elizabeth, are the prizes organized?"

Mr. Sloman looked toward his daughter at the far end of the school room, organizing the prize table, brimming with baby bottles, nipples, talcum powder, and chocolate – rare finds in the Canadian wilderness.

"Yes, Papa. I'm almost done."

Mr. Sloman stood, stretched, and poked his head outside the rail-car door.

"Billy! I'm ready to put the projector together! Do you want to help?"

Billy came running from behind the rail-car, out of breath, his face reddened and shining with tears.

"Papa! He's gone! He's gone!"

"Who's gone, son?" Mr. Sloman ran down the stairs and knelt in front of his son.

"Rudy! Rudy's gone! He ran off and I can't find him," Billy sobbed, his little shoulders heaving up and down.

Mr. Sloman tilted a sympathetic head and wrapped the boy in his arms.

"Aw, Billy, that's what foxes do. We knew we'd only keep him long enough for his leg to heal. You did such a good job getting him well, he felt strong enough to go home to the woods again."

"But he's my good ol' fox, Papa, and I'm gonna miss him."

"I know. I'll miss him too. He's a pretty nice fox, indeed."

Fredda ran towards the school-car with Petunia in her arms.

"What's wrong, Billy?"

"Rudy ran away. I can't find him," Billy sniffed.

"Petunia wanted to run away too, but I caught her." Fredda kissed the wiggly skunk.

"Petunia wants to go home, too, Fredda. Don't you think she probably misses her skunk friends and family?"

Papa, still kneeling down, reached over and scratched the little skunk on the head.

"But I will miss her."

"And she misses her friends the same way you will miss her. You need to think about it, okay?"

Fredda nodded, "Okay."

Mr. Sloman stood. "Now. Who wants to help me get the movie projector put together for tonight?"

"I do! I do!" sang the twins as they jumped up and down and ran to the school-car.

Inside, Mr. Sloman hooked the old film projector to a battery from a Model A Ford automobile. It gave power to the light bulb, but he had to turn the film by hand. Tonight, he would show a movie a friend sent him of his recent trip to Europe. He knew some of the families were homesick, and he was excited to surprise them with these pictures from their homeland.

Now that the snow had melted, some of the families arrived by canoe and others by hand-car. The hand-car was powered by a seesaw-like arm that people pumped up and down to move it along the railroad tracks. The Sloman children enjoyed playing with the car, but, for the people who had to pump the car for miles, it was exhausting work.

The evening was a success, and Mr. Sloman grew to know his families better through the games. Families wept when they watched the movie of his friend's European vacation, recognizing some of their hometowns. They pointed things out to their children and were excited to share with them the lands of their birth. Mr. Sloman's arm grew tired from winding the film backwards and forwards until everyone had seen their fill.

The next day was the last day of school for the year. Some of the families camped out beside the train or stayed with other families closer to the school-car. No one was late, even though the festivities of the night before had lasted well beyond bedtime.

The day was spent with Mr. Sloman assigning summer homework and loaning out lots of books. He never worried about them being returned. The families took exceptionally good care of the books, and he'd never had one unreturned.

Mr. Sloman was proud of his students. They had come to him speaking many languages other than English, and now most of the older students could already read from the Third Reader. At the end of the day, he wanted them to read something they would remember.

276

"Students, turn to page 137." Mr. Sloman opened his book without lifting his gaze.

"Everybody?" Joan usually didn't read out of the Third Reader.

"Yes, everyone. Today, on our last day of school and before saying good-bye, I want us to read something together."

A soft hush came over the school-car. The last day of school was sad for the children of the wilderness. Each month the school-car was the highlight of their lives. They didn't want to say good-bye.

They turned to their books and read:

A Song of Canada

Sing me a song of the great Dominion,
Soul felt words for a patriot's ear!
Ring out boldly the well-turned measure,
Voicing your notes that the world may hear:
Here is no starvalling—Heaven forsaken—
Shrinking aside where the nations throng.
Proud as the proudest moves she among them.
Worthy is she of a noble song.

A tear glimmered on Mr. Sloman's weathered cheek as he looked into the eyes of the children of the wilderness. These were the children of the very souls who were the backbone of Canada. Their families had sacrificed all to build in unchartered lands. He would miss them.

"Caw!" Jack broke the serious tone, flapping his wings.

Mr. Sloman laughed, "I think Jack agrees: Canada is indeed a noble land."

Author's Notes:

Before school-cars came to the wilderness, hundreds of children in Canada's isolated areas went without any formal education. They lived in remote areas where roads were few, and lakes, rivers, and streams were the main routes of transportation.

Mr. Fred Sloman, known as the "Dean of School Car Teachers," spent forty years on a little school-car between the years 1926-1965. He and his wife, Cela, raised five children and "train-car schooled" them.

Between 1926-1967, seven different school-cars served the wilderness children of Ontario. The Sloman school-car is now a museum in Clinton, Ontario, Canada.

TERRY FOX: CANADA'S HERO
JULY 28, 1958 -- JUNE 28, 1981

Somebody said it couldn't be done,

But he with a chuckle replied,

That "maybe it couldn't" but he would be one,

Who wouldn't say so till he'd tried.

~Edgar Allen Guest

September 1, 2011

Dear Pen-pal,

Greetings from the USA! I got your name today from my social studies teacher. My classmates and I are writing to people from other countries, and I decided to write to someone in Canada because our countries are neighbors. I drew a Canadian flag

279

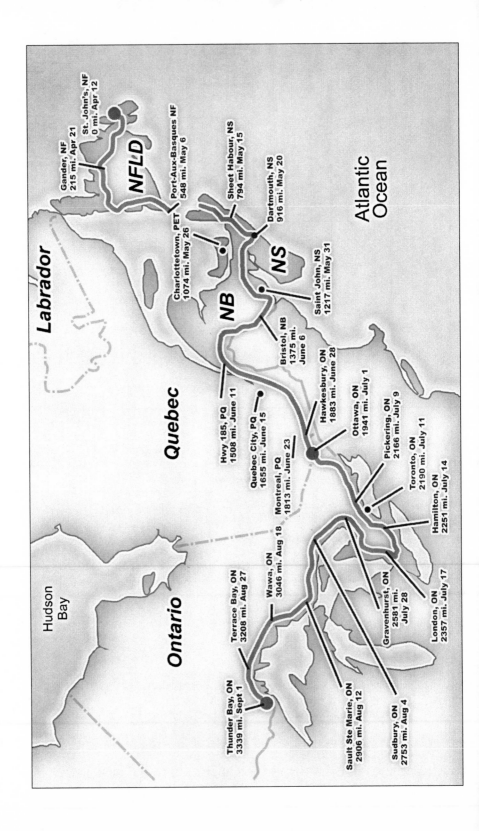

for you. I hope you like it.

Sincerely Yours,

Kayla, Indiana, USA

                                                    附

September 6, 2011

Dear Kayla,

Thanks for your letter. I'm glad we're pen-pals. I've always wanted to learn more about the United States. I like the stories about George Washington and Martin Luther King. Today, we got our pledge forms to raise money for Terry Fox. He's a hero like George Washington, except that he's Canadian. Terry Fox Day is so much fun–I can hardly wait! Our teacher said he will swallow a goldfish if we get the most pledges. Our principal promised to kiss a pig, if our school raises the most funds!

Last summer my dad shaved his legs for Terry Fox on Canada Day. My mom said I could dye my hair purple next year.

I'm sending you a picture my mom took of me standing in front of Niagara Falls while we were on vacation last year. Have you ever been there?

Write soon!

Sincerely Yours,

Camille, Manitoba, Canada

૪

September 7, 2011

Dear Camille,

Thanks for the picture of Niagara Falls. I've never been there.

Why is Terry Fox famous?

My Mom said I could send you a dollar for your fundraiser. If your teacher swallows a goldfish, will you take a picture and send it to me? Why did your dad shave his legs? And why do you dye your hair purple for Terry Fox? Did he like purple or something?

Your Friend,

Kayla

૪

September 14, 2011

Dear Kayla,

I'm sending you a booklet about Terry Fox. He was one cool dude. My grandma says he was a strong and beautiful young man. He's my hero. I want to dye my hair purple to raise money for him. That's why my Dad shaved his legs, too.

I hope you like the booklet.

Love,

Camille

Kayla looked at the picture of the young man on the front of the book. He was cute, with blue eyes, curly hair, and freckles, but something about his picture made her sad. How could this man make people celebrate, paint their hair purple, shave their legs, swallow goldfish, and kiss pigs?

She lay back on her pillow and began to read.

೫

Winnipeg, Manitoba 1960

"Terry! Terry, where are you?"

I heard my mother call my name. Out of the corner of my eye, I saw her peek around the corner and watch as I studied the wooden blocks strewn about the living room floor. In concentration, I stuck my tongue out and placed a block on top of the other three I had stacked earlier. They fell. Quick as a grasshopper, I picked up another block and began again. Over and over, I piled the blocks and never flinched when they fell. One block after another, I built a tower.

"You are a stubborn little fellow, Terry Fox. You've got Canadian grit and determination, I'll say that for you," Mother chuckled as she went back to cooking dinner. I never looked up to see her. I concentrated fully on my task.

In July of 1966, my family moved to Vancouver, British Columbia. At about ten years old, I was no less engrossed in play when I overheard my mother talking to my big sister.

"Judith, have you seen Terry?"

"He's playing table hockey, Mom."

I could hear my sister, Judith, setting the table.

"Can you get him and tell him to wash up for dinner?"

I could hear my mother's fried chicken sizzling on the stove.

"It won't do any good. He's stuck on that game."

Mother tiptoed down the basement stairs and peeked into the room. Out of the corner of my eye I saw her watch as I played table hockey for both teams. On the wall was a complicated diagram of an entire season's schedule I had drawn.

"Terry, what are you doing?"

"I gotta see who's gonna win," I spoke without looking up.

"How long before this game is over?" asked Mother, with a smile in her voice.

"One more shot."

WHACK! The puck went into the hole.

I walked to the wall and advanced one team to the next game and eliminated another.

"Who won?" Mom guided me up the stairs.

"Montreal," I shrugged, "but they're going up against Toronto next. It'll be a good game. What's for supper?"

Mom chuckled and led me to the kitchen, "Fried chicken. Go, wash up."

After washing my hands, I sat beside my father and next to my brother, Fred.

"Elbows off the table, Terry, and remove your hat."

My Mom frowned at my little brother, "You know the rules. Darrell, quit using your fingers. Use your knife and fork like your father."

Dad and Mom were particular about table manners.

After supper, I helped clear the table and went back to the basement to play. I bundled up carpets and made fortresses for my armies of cowboys, Indians and soldiers.

My little brother, Darrell, knelt down to study the formations.

"Can I play, Terry?"

"Sure. But remember, if a soldier is lying down with his face on the ground, he's dead; but if he's looking up, he's only wounded."

We played until the last man was down.

"Let's go and find Fred."

We picked up the toys and headed upstairs. We found Fred in his room doing homework. I tugged on his shirt sleeve.

"Fred, let's go and wrestle with Dad."

Fred put his pencil down and joined us in the living room, where we ganged up on our father.

"Oh, you want to wrestle, do you?"

Dad played as rough and tough as we did. That's why we liked it.

Pow! I threw a punch that landed on Dad's shoulder.

Thunk! Fred landed another one on his chest.

Wham! Dad let both of us have it on the ears.

We howled.

Our mother clucked her tongue, "I don't feel sorry for you.

You know it happens every time you rough-house with your father."

We jumped on Dad and wrestled some more. We were getting good licks in, and Dad popped us both on the shoulder.

Mom stood up from her chair.

"Okay, boys, time for bed. You have berry-picking tomorrow. You took the job, and you're going to keep it—no quitting."

We obeyed our mother. We were taught to respect our elders and do as we were told. Tomorrow we would pick berries to earn our own money for school-clothes and other things we wanted.

We ran to the bathroom to brush our teeth and shower.

"I'm going to pick enough berries for a ten-speed this year," Darrell boasted as he hopped into his PJ's.

"Not me! I'm getting golf clubs," Fred spoke through a mouth full of toothpaste.

"Me, too!" I zoomed out of the bathroom and landed in the middle of my bed. "I have baseball practice tomorrow."

The next day, after I got home from picking berries, I hurried into my baseball uniform and headed out the door an hour early.

"Why are you leaving so early, Terry? Stay home and play," Judith pouted as she stuck out her bottom lip.

"I can't! I don't want to miss my ride!"

CB

Grade Eight

My physical education teacher was Bob McGill. He stood at the front of the room while I swung my legs at the big desk. I was too short and my legs didn't reach the floor. A girl said hi to me and I ducked my head. I didn't know what to say to girls. I was too shy.

The teacher asked a question. I slunk down in my chair. *Please don't let him ask me, please. I'll just die.* I only got good grades to please my mother. I knew she cared, so I did my best to show her I could. I wanted to make her proud of me.

During regular classes I was shy, but in gym class, I was feisty and worked harder than any of the other kids. My best friend, Doug Alward, was shy, short, and loved basketball more than anything, just like me. But Doug was a much better athlete than I was. He was a cross-country runner and a first-string basketball player. I thought he was pretty cool.

For some reason, Coach McGill saw something in me.

"Terry, why don't you try out for cross-country running?"

Well, I have to tell you, running was not my thing, but Coach McGill was my hero and I would do anything for him. If he told me to swim across the ocean, I would do it. So, I tried out for cross-country. I hated it, except for one thing: every day after we finished running, Coach said, "Well done, men."

It made me feel so good to be called a man. I ran even harder the next day and the next day after that. I was just a skinny kid, but if

Coach saw me as a man, I could do anything for him.

"If you want something, you work for it, because I'm not interested in mediocrity," Coach said.

I still loved basketball the most. Everyone told me I was not made for it, but I ached to play. Coach suggested I try out for wrestling, but that was not my passion. I didn't care if I never got to play in a game. I went to every practice all year, and I only got to play for one minute the entire season.

"You're number 19 on a team of 19, Terry. Why don't you just go ahead and quit?" my teammates teased, trying to get me to give up, but I refused. Basketball was my passion.

One day, during the summer, between grades eight and nine, I called my best friend, Doug.

"Hey, Doug, let's go play one-on-one."

Doug paused.

"No thanks. I'm busy."

The next day, I called him again and suggested, "Let's play basketball."

I found out later that Doug didn't want to play with me because I was Canada's worst basketball player, but I wouldn't leave him alone, so he finally gave in. We played day after day, and Doug beat me every time. I didn't care. I loved to play, and I knew if I just kept trying I would improve.

Doug's older brother, Jack, a great basketball player, often joined us, too. When grade nine started, Jack and I went early to school to practise.

"Mom and Dad don't like me getting up early to play basketball." I passed the ball to Jack.

"Why not?" Jack took a shot.

I rebounded and passed it back to him. "They think I should sleep."

"So, how do you get here early, then?" Jack passed it to me.

"I wait until the very last minute to get out of bed. Then I run as fast as I can to get here in the dark."

I made a basket.

Even when I felt sick with the flu or a cold, I forced myself to my feet and ran to school.

I hung on Coach's every word: "If you want to be the best you have to get up early, practise before school, and stay late afterwards."

So that is exactly what I did.

Coach never cut anyone from the team, but he only played the twelve best players.

"Terry, you're one of the twelve this year," He confirmed as he slapped me on the shoulder.

"Really?"

I couldn't stop smiling.

"Yes. I've watched how hard you work. There are more talented players, but there aren't any harder workers. You never give up. You're the first to practise and the last to leave."

It meant so much to me to have Coach's approval that I worked harder to prove I was as good as he said. I had so much respect for Coach that, if he told me to hit my head against the wall, I would have. I believed Coach was the best leader on earth.

"I'll make you proud, Coach. I'll show you I'm good for something more than being laughed at by my teammates," I promised as I shook his hand with the firmest grip.

"I have no doubt you will, Terry."

By grade ten, Coach put me on the team as a starting guard, but in grade eleven, Doug and I went to separate schools. I joined the Port Coquitlam High School Ravens basketball team and scored twenty points in the first half of one game. I was shorter than the other guys, but I worked hard, even when our team got clobbered and there was no chance to win.

By 1976, when Doug and I played basketball, I could beat him. In grade twelve, both of us won Athlete of the Year. Doug and I were the best of friends. It was great having a friend who loved the same things I did. When he got a $2000 scholarship to university, he wrote the cheque out to me. He said I was a better athlete and more deserving, but I didn't agree. I returned the cheque to him and never forgot that kindness. Neither did my parents.

Doug and I drifted apart for a little while, and I started hanging out with other friends. Some of the guys I knew experimented with drugs like marijuana, but I never wanted to try them. Mostly, I just liked playing basketball, wrestling, joking around and playing hide-and-seek with my siblings.

290

I graduated from Port Coquitlam High School with all A's except for one B. My mom wanted me to go to college, so I enrolled at Simon Fraser University and decided to try out for the basketball team. I wanted to be a physical education teacher, like Coach McGill, and decided to major in kinesiology–the study of human movement.

During training camp I worked very hard. I had to: I was the smallest guy trying out again.

After a hard day of working out, Coach Delvin called me over to talk to me.

"We've been noticing you, Terry. You've made the team."

In the locker room I overheard Mike McNeill, one of the best players on the team talking, "Man, there are more talented players who didn't make the team, but Terry just out-gutted them. I have a lot of respect for that guy."

People asked me how I could push myself so hard. I think it's because I am mentally tough. I learned that kind of toughness running cross-country in junior high and by playing Doug one-on-one. I think I learned it from my siblings, when we wrestled with Dad on the couch and when we argued about who was the best player in the hockey league.

I loved to argue as much as my dad and brothers, but I could out-argue them. They would give up. I never would.

March 1, 1977

I loved playing basketball at university, but my leg began to hurt. I was sure it was the cartilage in my knee, so I ignored it as best as I could. I didn't want the coach to think I couldn't handle college basketball. But one morning I woke up and could not get out of bed.

That same day I got the kind of news that would strike fear in the toughest athlete: I had a malignant tumor. In four days, they would amputate my leg six inches above the knee.

I was only 18 years old, and I was going to lose my leg.

Everyone in my room cried. I knew it was up to me to make them feel better, and I made up my mind to be brave, but I admit, getting my leg cut off terrified me. Still, *I remember promising myself that if should I live, I would prove myself deserving of life.*[1]

When I first lost my leg I was in total shock because I was prepared for some type of operation to repair a cartilage or ligament problem in my knee. And I was not prepared for losing a leg. But it was a good thing for me because only two days later, I was shown an article of a man who ran on one leg and I'm a very competitive type of person. I said if he could do it, I could do it too, and right from the very beginning, I had the competitive attitude that I could beat my disability.

Within a few days of the amputation I began to think, *Okay. I've got one leg. What can I do with one leg? If I can get out and do something, I can give these people hope.*

Coach visited me in the hospital.

"How you feeling, Terry?"

I was determined not to feel sorry for myself.

"I'm great, Coach, but I won't be playing basketball any time soon."

Coach handed me a picture of Dick Trout, the man who ran the Boston Marathon on one leg.

That's when it popped into my head that I wanted to run across Canada. I decided after my year-and-a-half of chemotherapy, that I'd try and run across Canada and raise as much money as I could for the Canadian Cancer Society.

"Coach, I didn't understand that cancer hits young people. Young people are giving up. They aren't trying. But if this guy can do a marathon, so can I!" I pointed to the picture in my hand.

I went through months of chemo and radiation therapies and have never been so sick in my life. It was harder than any race I ever ran. Eventually, the day came to make my plans a reality.

The guy who made my prosthetic leg, Ben Speicher, did not have the kind of faith I had in myself.

"It's not feasible, Terry. It'll jar your stump and your whole body when you land on the leg."

"Anything's possible," I insisted.

Ben shook his head and sighed, "I've never had a patient who wanted to run a marathon."

"There's a first time for everything," I stated, hoping my determination didn't sound like bragging.

Once I got my prosthetic leg, it felt like I was walking on air—and not in a good way. I wanted to start training for my run across Canada, so in February I called my old coach, Bob McGill.

"Coach, will you help me? I want to see if I can run on this thing."

After some small talk, we met at the university track.

Coach motioned me forward.

"Let's start moving and see what happens."

By the time I ran one hundred meters, my stump was bleeding. I fell down and got up over and over again.

As Coach helped me, a woman, who was watching her sons play soccer in another field, came running toward us, screaming like a mad-woman and pointing at me hysterically.

"Get that freak out of here!"

I was too embarrassed to go back to the track in the daytime, so I trained by going out at night. *I trained as hard as I thought you could train for it. Before Christmas I ran 101 days in a row without taking a day off. In that time I ran with the flu, shin splints, bone bruises--you name it, I had it. And I ran through it for all that time because I felt I had to build my confidence for my trip. I knew when I ran across Canada, I would encounter the same obstacles.*

I could not do this marathon alone: I needed someone to accompany me; and to follow me, I needed a vehicle that I could use as a place to sleep. So, I wrote to Ford Canada and asked them to loan me a van. Right away, they agreed to loan me a nice Econoline

Funcraft. It had a bench inside on which I could sleep, a small table, and a cassette deck. There were tiny cupboards and a two-toned carpet. It also had a small stove and fridge. There was even a toilet.

I also wrote to the Canadian Cancer Society:

October 1979

> *The night before my amputation, my former basketball coach brought me a magazine with an article on an amputee who ran in the New York Marathon. It was then I decided to meet this new challenge head-on and not only overcome my disability, but conquer it in such a way that I could never look back and say it disabled me.*

> *But I soon realized that would only be half my quest, for as I went through the sixteen months of the physically- and emotionally-draining ordeal of chemotherapy, I was rudely awakened by the feelings that surrounded and coursed through the cancer clinic. There were faces with brave smiles, and ones who had given up smiling. There were feelings of hopeful denial and the feelings of despair. My quest would not be a selfish one. I could not leave knowing these faces and feelings would still exist, even though I would be set free from mine. Somewhere the hurting must stop... and I was determined to take myself to the limit*

for this cause.

From the beginning, the going was extremely difficult, and I was facing chronic ailments foreign to runners with two legs, in addition to the common physical strains felt by all dedicated athletes.

But these problems are now behind me, as I have either out-persisted or learned to deal with them. I feel strong, not only physically, but, more importantly, emotionally. Soon I will be adding one full mile a week, and, coupled with the weight training I have been doing, by next April I will be ready to achieve something that for me was once only a distant dream reserved for the world of miracles – to run across Canada to raise money for the fight against cancer.

The running I can do, even if I have to crawl every last mile.

We need your help. The people in cancer clinics all over the world need people who believe in miracles.

I am not a dreamer, and I am not saying that this will initiate any kind of definitive answer or cure to cancer, but I believe in miracles – I have to.

Terry Fox, 1979

My training continued. *I took it right from the first as a challenge. I had a lot of help from friends and relatives.*

296

I ran over 3000 miles. I trained hard, and I was really motivated to set an example for people with disabilities. There are two groups of people with disabilities: one group that feels sorry for themselves, gets depressed, and crawls in a hole; and another group that takes a disability as a challenge, and they're very healthy. I wanted to set an example of how one can approach life.

I really didn't know what cancer was all about until I had it, and I went through a year-and-a-half of chemotherapy treatments during which I lost my hair temporarily. I was very sick and unhealthy, but to other cancer patients, I was very healthy. It had a real impact on me, living with people who are dying and very sick and unhealthy, and this was a big motivational reason for running. By running, I could really set an example for these people.

My artificial leg attached to my leg by suction. They do not build legs for running. The leg I had was a walking leg. I had to take an extra little hop with my good leg in order to run. It was a tiring and exhausting technique. In the beginning it was very hard on my good leg. I went through periods of shin splints. I lost toe nails. Sores came and went from friction and from sweat. I learned to deal with it.

In the beginning of the marathon, *I hoped to start off around 30 miles* [a day] *and build up to 35 or 40 along the way.*

During training *my* [artificial] *leg broke down like you would not believe. Every week-and-a-half, a knee* [would] *go or my foot would break off because they* [were not] *built for running. I have three legs altogether and a couple of knees and spare parts, but it was a problem I had to deal with. At least I could replace my knee, and you cannot.*

When I started the run, I hoped to get home by September or October.

⁍

The Marathon of Hope Begins

April 12, 1980

My best friend, Doug Alward, agreed to drive the van for me. We packed eight pairs of running shoes and three extra legs. Other people had run across Canada, but they had not included Newfoundland in their runs. I wanted to start in Newfoundland at the Atlantic Ocean.

On April 12, 1980, at 2:45 PM, in St. John's Harbor, Doug and I went to the shore of the Atlantic and filled two large, clear bottles with water from the ocean: one for a souvenir and the other to empty into the Pacific Ocean at the end of my run, at Vancouver's Stanley Park.

Finally, it was time to begin. I dipped my prosthetic leg into the Atlantic and began the Marathon of Hope. Doug drove a mile ahead of me to mark my miles. There were not very many people there that day to watch my start. Since it was Saturday, the Canadian Broadcast System (CBC) did not want to pay a reporter overtime, but they sent a cameraman. He sat in the trunk of a car that drove beside me while I ran.

My prosthetic leg was just a little too long to swing behind me without a little extra hop. *Some people couldn't figure out what I was doing. It wasn't a walk-hop; it wasn't a trot; it was running, or as close as I could get to running, and it was harder than doing it on two legs. It made me mad when people called it a walk. If I was walking, it wouldn't have been anything.*

It may not have looked like I was running fast, but I was going as hard as I could. It bothered me, people coming up beside me. I wanted to make those guys work. I couldn't stand making it easy for them. I was really competitive. When they ran with me, they usually ran for only two or three miles; for me, it might have been my twenty-sixth mile.

Physically it was tough, but it was mainly a mental battle... like going through the cancer treatments. Going through all that was entirely mental. It didn't matter what physical problems I had because I'd been running through shin-splints and bone-bruises and sores and even the flu. It was only because I was mentally set that I was able to go through it. It's something anybody can do, if they're strong enough in their mind.

I liked to [run] 12 miles and then take a break and then do another 10 more and take a break. By then, I was really dead-tired but then I liked to do at least three more. I never went under 25 miles in a day.

When I started the run, I said that if we [all Canadians] gave one dollar, we'd have $22 million for cancer research, and I didn't care, man, there was no reason that wasn't possible. No reason. I wasn't doing the run to become rich or famous. If anyone gave a dollar, they were a part of the Marathon of Hope.

I just really wanted to send a message that *whatever you do you've got to do the best you can possibly do. I told the public: "I'm going to do everything I can. If I don't make it, it's going to be something where nobody would make it."*

I ran from the harbour to City Hall, where they had me wear the mayor's cloak-of-office and raise the flag of the Cancer Society. From there, I continued to run through Newfoundland. In Gander, *people came and lined up and gave me ten, twenty bucks just like that. And that's when I knew that the Run had unlimited potential. On May 6, I ran in Port-Aux-Basques, population 10,000, and raised $10,000, equal to one dollar per person.*

But the run had *been really tough because, for one, our van broke down. We got snowed in one day, and another day the wind was bad. A CBC van was filming me, and a big freight truck came up from behind and rammed into the CBC vehicle at about 50 miles an hour and forced it off the road and into the ditch. If I hadn't been where I was, the CBC van would have hit me.*

During the first month of the run, I wrote in my journal:

> **"April 26, 1980; 337 miles, day 15**
>
> *"Today we got up at 4:00 AM. As usual, it was tough. We drove the 35 miles back to the starting point,*

and I took off again. Later the valve system on my leg
completely eroded away; I got many sores from this, so
I had to convert over to my spare leg."

"Tuesday, April 29th, 1980; Day 18; 25 miles total;
412 miles; Psalm 35

    "It was another one of those days when nothing
was organized, so we raised very little money. In a
town of 5,000, nobody came to meet us."

We didn't know it would still be winter in Newfoundland. We lived in the van a lot. The first day the heater did not work, and we froze. I knew what it would be like to run, but not what it would be like to not have any solace, living in the van. By the fourth week, Doug and I were not getting along. I was glad to go to sleep every night. Above my bunk, I taped a poem written by Edgar Guest. I read it before I went to sleep, and I read each morning when I awoke:

It Couldn't Be Done
by Edgar Allan Guest
Somebody said it couldn't be done,
But he with a chuckle replied,
That "maybe it couldn't", but he would be one,
Who wouldn't say so till he'd tried.
So he buckled right in, with the trace of a grin, on his face.

If he worried he hid it.

He started to sing and he tackled the thing,

That couldn't be done, and he did it.

Somebody scoffed: Oh you'll never do that;

At least no one has ever done it.

But he took off his coat and he took off his hat,

And the first thing we knew he's begun it.

With a lift of his chin, and a bit of a grin,

Without any doubting or quiddit,

He started to sing and he tackled the thing,

That couldn't be done, and he did it.

There are thousands to tell you it cannot be done,

There are thousands to prophesy failure;

There are thousands to point out to you, one by one,

The dangers that wait to assail you.

But just buckle right in with a bit of a grin,

Just take off your coat and go to it;

Just start to sing as you tackle the thing

That "cannot be done", and you'll do it.

I couldn't forget that there were kids in the hospital suffering with cancer that might not make it, kids my age and younger, kids that were healthy when I started, healthier than me, and had died by the time I was done with my treatment. You just can't leave something like that and try and forget it. I couldn't, anyway.

Still, those first weeks were very hard and lonely: snow storms, ferocious winds, and two guys living together in a van. We got on each other's nerves. *I was very sore and tired. I had some chafing problems on my stump, and I'd been running into the wind which I found really draining. But I had unbelievable support from the public. It was tremendous. When you get that kind of support you don't feel pain.*

I pushed on through Eastern Canada and stayed in touch with CBC Radio to keep the public posted on my run. I emphasized the need for people to get involved in my interviews:

"There are 25 million people who live in Canada. Each one of us 25 million can get cancer. None of us is immune. And each one of us has a dollar to give, each one of us and more. Most of us have more. Don't tell me that we can't raise 25 million dollars from the public of Canada. Don't tell me that. I've got to set my goals high. Because nobody said I could run across Canada, I'm gonna give everything I've got to make it. Now I've got the chance and I'm gonna set my goals high. I believe in miracles--I have to. And there's no reason why we can't raise that kind of money, and I hope you'll respond; I hope you'll all do your part; and

*I hope you'll talk to people and motivate them, because
I know we can all give a dollar."*

By May 14, I had run 767 miles. I wrote in my journal: *"Now
carrying my own water bottle when I run and making my own lunches.
Doug won't do a thing for me."*

There were lots of disagreements between us. I realized we
needed another person to help us get through this. On May 31, after
running 1,217 miles, my little brother, *Darrell, arrived, and it was very
heartwarming to see him. We burned a few tears as we embraced. It
got me moving a bit faster.*

I needed Darrell's sense of humour. He also helped Doug by
driving, doing laundry, and taking care of other details. Darrell could
have gone back to sleep every morning when I started my run, but he
never did. He said as long as I was out there working, he would work
too.

He asked Doug how he could stand to watch me do this day
after day and Doug just answered, "I don't. I couldn't take it if I did."

I guess it was hard to watch.

By June 1, I had run 1,240 miles, and *it was boiling hot. I got
very tired, and the miles went slowly. I took a break and tried again,
but only managed one mile.*

By this time, the Canadian Cancer Society saw I was getting a
lot of attention, so they assigned me a publicist. Bill Vigars was my
Public Relations guy who organized the press.

On May 15, I arrived in Sheet Harbour, Nova Scotia, and, after a reception for me there, I ran with some school children: *When I ran with the kids I really burned it just to show them how fast I could go. They were tired and puffing.* On May 20, in Dartmouth, *I ran to the vocational school with fifty students. I ran about a mile. They had raised about $3,000. What a great group of kids!*

By May 26, I was in Charlottetown, Prince Edward Island: *There were lots of people out to cheer me on and support me. Incredible! I had another dizzy spell during the run. It was still freezing, but I wasn't wearing sweats, so people could see my leg. I'd run just over twenty-eight miles* by the time I ran through town there.

In New Brunswick, not very many people seemed to know about the Marathon of Hope:

We learned that Saint John would have nothing organized for us. I tried so hard and then got let down. I decided to run right down the city's main street. Doug followed behind and honked. We were rebels, stirring up noise. People knew Terry Fox ran out of his way to Saint John for a reason!

Every day I got up early in the morning and ran. At times, *the first few miles were the usual torture. My foot blistered badly, but my stump wasn't too bad. In some towns I had tremendous support. Everybody honked and waved, looked out of their homes and stores, and cheered me on. In Perth-Andover, New Brunswick, there was tremendous support and it quickened up my pace for the remaining fourteen miles. I flew!*

On Highway 185, in Quebec, the wind howled in my face all day. It was very difficult, constantly running into the wind. It zapped [strength] *right out of my body and head. The only people there who knew about the Run were the truckers and the out-of-province people. Everyone else wanted to stop and give me a lift. On Highway 20, I was tired and weary because people were continually forcing me off the road. People passed from behind me on this narrow road. It was so frustrating.*

ೞ

By the time I reached Quebec City, people were catching on to my vision. I was honored by meeting Gérard Côté, a four-time Boston Marathon winner! They featured me on the front page of the French-language daily, *Le Soleil*.

In Montreal, I ran into the city with Alouette kicker, Don Sweet, and four wheelchair-athletes. There was a band of two hundred playing and thousands of balloons, and, in Hawkesbury, Ontario, a huge sign greeted me that read "WELCOME TERRY. YOU CAN DO IT!"

In Ottawa, I learned they wanted me to kick the opening ball of the Canada Football League exhibition game between Ottawa and Saskatchewan. I realized I had finally gotten my message to most of Canada when 16,000 people gave me a standing ovation, after I kicked the ball with my good leg.

Within four to five days, it went from people honking at me in order to drive me off the road, to people slowing down and handing me money. I was exhausted from a run in Millwood and collapsed in my van, but in my hand I held a wrinkled $100 bill someone had handed me on the run. It felt good.

Later, I heard that, when I was in Pickering, a couple named John and Edna Neale waited hours for me to pass by. When they finally saw me, they said, "He was just what was needed to give us a little pride in our own people, the same kind Americans have in abundance."

I knew I was becoming more visible to the public, but I do not think I realized the magnitude of my popularity, until I arrived at the Scarborough Civic Center in Ontario and saw six or seven hundred people waiting to see me. I walked into the atrium and saw it jammed with people eight or nine stories high. Someone held up a sign that read, "Every Mile Wins a Smile."

People said Canada had never seen anyone like me and that I was uniting Canada like no one else before me, but the only part of this publicity I cared about was *to know that Cancer can be beaten.*

In Toronto, people followed me on bikes, people with cameras ran with me, and thousands lined the streets and shoved money into the donation bag. Women even ran out of the hair salons with curlers in their hair. I gave a speech to more than 10,000 people. My Dad was so proud of me he tried to hold my arm up in the air, but I would not let him. I did not like my dad raising my arm. I just wanted to raise money for a cure to cancer.

Photo: Wikimedia / Public Domain / Terry Fox in Toronto taken by Jeremy Gilbert

I did not really know what to say to the crowds—I was overwhelmed—but they wanted me to speak, so I said, *"Treating me like I'm something above other people: I've never been treated like*

308

this before. It almost hurts me. "

Now that I was truly well-known, everyone wanted me to speak and appear. It was mid-summer, 90 degrees, the humidity was stifling, and I had three speaking engagements or receptions each day, in addition to running a marathon. Still, it was worth it because people would run alongside of me on the highways and hand me money. Large corporations joined my cause and donated funds too.

The stinky, little toilet in our van was a mixed blessing. We could not get the stench out of it, and the only way to empty it was to lift it out of the van and shake it, which caused its contents to splatter all over us. But as I began the run and people began to know who I was, its unpleasant odor actually worked in my favour by keeping away unwanted visitors. It gave me a refuge from the crowds. I could be thankful even for a smelly van.

But I did love hearing from the people, and their encouragement kept me going. They helped me remember why I was putting myself through this.

One mom approached me and said, "You're running for my son."

"Where is he?" I looked into the crowd to see if anyone joined her.

"He died last week."

Every day, people put their hope and sadness onto me, and I felt it. It was what kept me going. There had to be a cure.

The muscles in my leg and my right arm became sore because I hadn't run up and down hills in a long time. On August 27, I read the Doug Collins [article] *which said that I rode through Quebec.*

I called the guy who wrote the article lying about me.

"Why would you write this? You ruined the whole run. You destroyed it. You told people I didn't do it."

I was very discouraged. I had run and suffered through every single mile. I would never deceive the public like that.

But the next day, I had a *good 13-mile run in the morning. The weather was perfect: no wind and cold. In the afternoon my ankle started to hurt again.*

The Canadian Cancer Society called me and asked if a 10-year-old boy named Greg Scott could spend some time with me on my run. Greg had the same kind of cancer I had and had one of his legs amputated, too: *Greg rode his bike behind me for about six miles, and it was the most inspirational moment I'd had. At night we had a beautiful reception in Terrace Bay. I spoke about Greg and couldn't hold back the emotion when I spoke:*

> *'After the operation is when I started to go*
> *through my chemotherapy and drug treatments. I'll*
> *tell you right now that a lot of people say I need*
> *courage and guts and stamina to run across Canada*
> *on one leg, but the courage I needed to get through*
> *that was way worse. It was unreal; I'll never forget it.*
> *I'm crying now because there's somebody here right*

now who is going through the same thing that I went through—the exact same thing and he's only ten years old. I had the most inspirational day of my life today.'

I hadn't been swimming since I had my leg amputated, but I jumped in the lake for Greg. That little boy represented why I was doing the marathon. Spending time with him took me back to the hospital's cancer-ward.

Shortly after Greg spent time with me, he died.

On September 1, people were still lining the road saying to me, 'Keep going; don't give up; you can do it; you can make it; we're all behind you.' Well, you don't hear that and have it go in one ear and out the other.

I was feeling pretty good in the morning and things were going nicely. All of a sudden I saw eight pictures of everything. I was dizzy and light-headed. Was it all over? Is everything finished? Had I let everyone down? I had a hacking cough and thought it was a cold.

I needed to see a doctor. I thought I might be running my last mile: *There was a camera crew waiting at the three-quarter mile point to film me. I don't think they even realized that they filmed my last mile... people were still saying, 'You can make it all the way, Terry.'*

I had run 3,339 miles in 143 days and had raised two million dollars.

After I saw the doctor, the news was not good: I had a tumor the size of a lemon and another the size of a golf ball in my lungs. The next day I spoke to the press, while lying on a gurney on my way into the ambulance:

> *"Yesterday I was running and I had noticed a little bit of hardness of breathing. And near the end of the day, at 18 miles, I was coughing and choking and had pain in my neck and my chest and did three more miles and decided I needed to go to the doctor and it was discovered then. Originally, I had primary cancer in my knee, three-and-a-half years ago. The cancer has spread, and now I've got cancer in my lungs, and we've got to go home and try to do some more treatment. All I can say is, if there's any way I can get out there again and finish it, I will.*
>
> *"Even if I'm not running anymore, we've still got to try and find a cure, and I think other people should try to get ahead and do their thing now. As I've been preaching all along, all the way through Canada, to people who have cancer: I'm not going to give up; I'm going to fight and I'm going to do everything I can. I hope that what I've done has been an inspiration, and I hope that I will see people take off where I've left off here."*

At a press conference the next day, I said:

"I don't feel that this is unfair. That's the thing about cancer: I'm not the only one. It happens all the time to people. I'm not special. This just intensifies what I did. It gives it more meaning. It'll inspire more people... I just wish people would realize that anything's possible if you try. When I started this run, I said that if we all gave one dollar, we'd have $22 million for cancer research, and I don't care, man, there's no reason that isn't possible--no reason.

"I'm not bitter at anybody or anything. To me, I'm happy with what I've done. I've done my best. You can make your own opinion on what you think I've done."

My Dad was very upset.

"This is so unfair; this is so unfair."

"No it isn't, Dad; I'm just like everybody else."

Out of the blue, one of the television networks decided to do a telethon. The entire nation of Canada was behind me. It was the most powerful, unifying experience Canadians had ever experienced.

That night I went to the hospital. When the telethon was halfway through, I started my chemotherapy treatment: *I'd have rather been out on the road running across Canada. Now I just sat there and hoped and prayed that it would all work out alright for the best.*

On September 19, 1980, His Excellency the Governor General Ed Schreyer traveled to my hometown to present me with the Order of Canada, Canada's highest civilian honor. In his speech he said, "You have indeed succeeded in helping to build a better country and helping to evoke a better spirit and mood that we can all agree we can call our finest effort. I call to mind *Conscripted Dream*: 'Great soul that took the long and painful road and helped create a dream that could not fail.'

"By his disregard for his own pain and by his devotion to a great cause, Terry embodies the motto of the order of Canada: 'Desiderantes meliorem patriam—they desired a better country.'"

∞

Good-bye, Dear Son of Canada

June 28, 1981

One month before his twenty-third birthday, Terry Fox died peacefully at Royal Columbian Hospital in New Westminster, British Columbia. The press was greeted solemnly by the Deputy Director of Nursing, Alison Stinson.

"Terry has completed the last kilometre of his marathon. A short time ago, he died. He died surrounded by love--the love of his family, all of whom were with him, and the love and prayers of the entire nation. He has left us a legacy of hope, which I think will live and become a part of our nation's heritage. He was a friend and I'm going to miss him."

314

Terry had left such an impression on Canada that government buildings flew their flags at half-mast—an honour usually reserved for distinguished statesmen and politicians.

Canada mourned the loss of a great Canadian son, but Terry's life and death were not in vain.

On Sept. 19, 2010, the 30th annual *Terry Fox Run* was held. Terry's *Marathon of Hope* continues and, so far, has raised $553 million for cancer research. In 2008 alone, more than two million people in twenty-eight countries took part in Terry Fox runs. Those countries included Afghanistan, Vietnam, Saudi Arabia, Oman, Malaysia, France, Belgium, and the United States.

β

October 1, 2011

Dear Camille,

Thanks for sending me that booklet on Terry Fox. He was your hero, and now he's mine. I'm going to ask my mom if we can celebrate Terry Fox Day now too. I cried when I read it, because he was so strong and brave and helped so many people.

I'll write more later. I have to study for a test. Ugh–math!

Your Friend,

Kayla

October 18, 2011

Dear Kayla,

I've enclosed a flyer from my school about Terry Fox Day. I hope your school can have Terry Fox Day too.

And don't worry about the test. Just remember what Terry always said:

"It's okay, just do your best."

Your Friend,

Camille

Endnotes:

[1]From this point on, all words in italics are direct quotes of Terry Fox retrieved from the CBC [Canadian Broadcasting Corporation] Digital Archives, used here with their kind permission. You can visit CBC on the web at http://archives.cbc.ca/sports/exploits/topics/71

About the Author:

Karla Akins is a pastor's wife, mother of five, and grandma to five beautiful little girls. She lives in North Manchester, Indiana with her husband, twin teenage boys with autism, and three crazy dogs. Her favorite color is purple, favorite hobby is books, and favorite food group is cupcakes. You can contact Karla via her website at www.KarlaAkins.com

Other books in this series:

What *Really* Happened in Ancient Times
What *Really* Happened During the Middle Ages
What *Really* Happened in Colonial Times

PDF e-books available at
www.bramleybooks.com

Kindle e-books available at
www.amazon.com

CPSIA information can be obtained at www.ICGtesting.com
Printed in the USA
BVOW032108270911

272241BV00003B/2/P

9 781932 786453